Build *for* Tomorrow

Build *for* Tomorrow

Jason Feifer

HARMONY

BOOKS · NEW YORK

Copyright © 2022 by Jason Feifer

Published in the United States by Harmony Books,
an imprint of Random House, a division of
Penguin Random House LLC, New York.
harmonybooks.com

Harmony Books is a registered trademark, and the Circle colophon is
a trademark of Penguin Random House LLC.

Library of Congress Cataloging-in-Publication Data
CIP data is available upon request.

ISBN 978-0-593-23538-6
Ebook ISBN 978-0-593-23539-3

Printed in the United States of America
Text Designer: Andrea Lau
Jacket Designer: Anna Bauer

10 9 8 7 6 5 4 3 2 1

First Edition

Contents

Build *for* Tomorrow

Introduction

We are in a time of great change. Warp-speed innovations are changing how we work, shop, and socialize; millions of people are rethinking their careers; businesses are scrambling to meet consumers' new expectations; cultural shifts have given us new words, new relationships, and a new awareness; and of course, we will long be grappling with the results of a global pandemic. But while these are big things, they're felt in small and personal ways. We are asking ourselves heavy questions about what we desire, and where we find opportunity, and what we're willing to sacrifice. All of us have and will experience change that has absolutely nothing to do with the rest of the world—changes to our friendships, families, homes. Your life, exactly as you know it now, will not exist in a few years. It's a guarantee.

So, what can you do about it? Through my role as editor in chief of *Entrepreneur* magazine, I speak to founders, innovators, and businesspeople of all stripes, from mom-and-pop store owners to the heads of multinational corporations, as well as the people in the weeds who make the smartest companies smarter. They're people you've never heard of, and some of the most famous names in the world. But they all have one thing in common—they are good at change. And no matter their size or scale or income level, they all seem to have gone through the same four distinct phases as they experience and value change. These phases also line up with what we all have gone through together over the past few years as our collective world shifted.

The first is the most familiar . . .

Panic!

Absolute, total panic. Our lives became unfamiliar. Our futures became unknowable. Planning felt impossible. And then, phase two . . .

Adaptation

The dust began to clear. We saw what was now possible, and what was not. We began to work with what we had. And then, phase three . . .

New Normal

We got comfortable again, like settling into a pair of new shoes. We established new rules, though we still longed for the old ones. And then, finally, although it may have been slow, we began to reach . . .

Wouldn't Go Back

When I say "wouldn't go back," I do not mean to discount the loss and suffering that so many people experience—either during Covid, or as a result of any other change. When industries shift and factories close, suffering results. When personal relationships fall apart, or lives or are lost, the emptiness and loneliness can feel inescapable. This is real.

But still, I am here to tell you this: Something recently forced these people to make a change—and although it was painful and disorienting at first, it ultimately pushed them to rethink their lives and businesses in a positive way. A landscape painter named Meg O'Hara articulated that shift nicely. She told me about how she once made a living doing commissioned paintings for ski resorts—but when travel shut down in the early days of the pandemic, her business evaporated. She was in her twenties and had just built this career; now she imagined it being over. "I stepped back and let myself freak out for twenty-four or forty-eight hours, drank a little wine, and then said, OK, some of the greatest ideas are going to come out of this time," she told me. "If there was ever going to be an opportunity for me to pivot in an interesting direction, maybe it's now." She started marketing her work to individual skiers, worked hard to build relationships with them, and as a result doubled her revenue, was able to hire her first employee, and won a local "30 Under 30" award. "My business has fundamentally changed. I don't think I can go back," O'Hara said. I hear people tell similar stories about more personal changes as well—the woman whose agonizing divorce pushed her to rebuild her social life and create a thriving consulting business; the overworked executive who stepped down from a job that he now admits he wasn't the right fit for, and now has more time for the things he really enjoys; and the couple who agonized over whether to move their family from Florida to Colorado, changed their minds multiple times, and finally did it—and are grateful they did. All these people rethought their habits and relationships and what was most important to them. They came away transformed for the better—and even if they could, they *wouldn't go back* to a time before they had this new change.

That's what I mean by Wouldn't Go Back. It's the most important of the four phases. It's the entire point of the four phases! Some of us are already there; some are not. Even when we get there, a new change may set us back to Panic, and we start all over again. But our goal, collectively, should be to continually move toward Wouldn't Go Back—because that's when we can start recognizing and collaborating on the opportunities of tomorrow, and stop wasting our energy trying to re-create the past. It is the reason I'm writing this book: I want to help you reach Wouldn't Go Back. It begins by recognizing that our actions today are building for tomorrow.

This is a book for absolutely anyone facing down an uncertain future, as well as a practical guide for every entrepreneur and aspiring entrepreneur who hopes to help shape the world. As we reach a critical crossroads in history, we must accept that the future is not optional. We can't opt out of it. In business, culture, and politics, incumbents will fall and new challengers will rise up. The results will be unpredictable, but as individuals, we cannot slow or stop it. We *can,* however, participate in it and benefit from it.

I understand this isn't easy. When I started at *Entrepreneur* magazine in 2015, I wasn't comfortable with change. I had taken risks during my career, but they were always in a safe, narrow space. I had an unchanging vision of my purpose, my abilities, and my direction. Then I started talking to professional innovators, and I discovered an entirely new way of thinking. Entrepreneurs are adaptable in a way I didn't think possible; they seemed to have an intuitive understanding of what is important and worth protecting, and what could be discarded into the ocean like a rocket ship's booster. I'd never considered myself an entrepreneur before, but after a few years of these conversations, I started applying the word to myself. I also started to define entrepreneur differently. It wasn't a particular job or income level. The definition was simple: *An entrepreneur is someone who makes things happen for themselves.*

I don't care what kind of career you have. I don't care if you work for someone else, or for yourself, or for nobody. If you make things happen for yourself, or if you aspire to do so, then I am talking to you right now. This thinking applies to you. Because even as we all build something for ourselves, we must remember that we're building on shifting ground. Our foundation will be rocked. We cannot anticipate tomorrow's needs, but we can anticipate that tomorrow *will* have needs, and they *will* be different from today's. We must start to see instability as a form of opportunity.

In the spring of 2020, during the early days of the Covid pandemic, I witnessed just how powerful this mode of thinking could be. Even as the world seemed to crumble, entrepreneurs began telling me about how they were making valuable changes to their businesses and lives. They were quickly running out of cash, and things they'd spent years building were coming crashing down, but they were on their toes—the woman who turned her spa into a cannabis dispensary called Hempress Farms, or the brand Goldens' Cast Iron, which started manufacturing home gym equipment alongside its existing line of grills and fire pits. In short, they were doing anything and everything to identify and solve new problems. I watched this and I wondered: *How will their story end?*

Back then, of course, there was no way to know what would happen to them. Were they correct or foolish? Was it worth being nimble, or should they have just given up and counted their losses? Only time would tell—which got me wondering about the past. Things like this had happened before, so what were the results?

I actually spend a lot of time with this question in my work researching and hosting the podcast *Build for Tomorrow*. The show explores how moments of great change happened throughout history, and how they shape our lives today. I'm continually looking for (and expanding upon in this book) the common threads between the past and the present—to see how a complete cycle of history played out before our time, and then use it to better understand the challenges and opportunities of today.

That's why, in the early days of the pandemic in 2020, as I struggled to understand how some saw so much potential in the middle of a pandemic, I called up a medieval historian to ask if anything good came out of the absolute worst version of a pandemic that I could think of—and that, of course, was the bubonic plague of the 1300s. I knew it killed a lot of people. But I didn't know what came next.

Did anything good really come from the bubonic plague?

The answer to that question helped me fully appreciate the moment that we're in right now. Because the lesson of that time, just like the lesson of today, is this: The moments of greatest change can also be the moments of greatest opportunity.

Our moment is now—if only we're willing to seize it.

The Good That Comes from Bad

You may remember the first part of this from grade school history class. Medieval Europe was an agricultural society with strict layers of hierarchy. Among the tiers: The lords owned the land, and the serfs were their slaves.

Then the year 1348 arrived, and the bubonic plague broke out in Europe. At first, that plague may not have seemed unusual. Cyclical diseases were more common back then. The rich were often able to leave for the countryside, waiting out the disease while the poor suffered and died. But the bubonic plague turned out differently. It killed upwards of 60% of Europe. Rich, poor, lords, serfs—nobody was spared.

After the worst of it, the lords of course wanted to get their businesses back up and running. They went to their serfs and said: *Get back to work!* But something was different. Many serfs had died, and there were no longer enough of them for all the lords. This meant the lords had to compete to hire the best labor. "These people who had been serfs, who had been basically slaves, suddenly find their labor in demand—and they can ask for actual compensation for it," said Andrew Rabin, a medieval scholar and professor of English at the University of Louisville, when I asked him whether anything good came from this plague. "Because you know, the lord of the manor next door is trying to get the serfs to *his* manor, and is offering incentives to do so."

This, Professor Rabin told me, was the very beginning of the employment contract as we know it: It codified the concept that labor has a value, and the people who provide that labor should be compensated for it. Some slaves returned to the land, but others said, screw it—I work for nobody. Then they moved to the city and started selling cloth and textiles, or transporting food and wine, or trading spices or cookware, or opening banks. They formed the first true merchant class. *All this* was the good that came out of the bubonic plague. It is, functionally speaking, the reason that I am writing this book (I got paid!) and that you are reading this book (to help you get paid more!). We have the bubonic plague to thank for this.

Of course, 60% of Europe died for us to achieve that. It was an unthinkable loss. And what followed was not an easy or peaceful transition. Still, would we want to go back to a time before the bubonic plague? Before the modern economy as we know it? This is an epic Wouldn't Go Back moment.

What causes massive shifts like this? Why *is* crisis such a creator of opportunity? Brian Berkey, an assistant professor in the legal studies and business ethics department at the Wharton School at the University of Pennsylvania, offers a simple but profound explanation: "A crisis like this can shift the window on the options that we are willing to collectively take seriously."

In other words, a crisis does not create new options. New opportunities are not beamed down from Mars; they don't come from nowhere. Instead, like remote work, they were always available—always waiting for us, always possible, but we just didn't take them seriously before. This is the downside of stability: We get comfortable with one way of doing things, and we are therefore not incentivized to find other ways to do these same things—even though those other ways might be better, smarter, more humane, more efficient, and more profitable. Moments of change, hard as they may be, are the things that force us onto higher ground.

Here's a small example. Leigh Ann Cannady founded the Forsyth Academy of Performing Arts in Georgia, where she and her team teach theater to kids. Their class sizes have always been large, because Cannady believed that was better for students and also made more economic sense for her school. But in order to make things safer during the pandemic, she shrank the class sizes—assuming it would be a temporary change made under duress. Instead, she was shocked by the result: People preferred smaller classes! Teachers were less stressed and students got more individualized attention. Her school even made the same exact amount of money as with larger classes, because smaller classes are easier to fill up, which means she didn't need to spend as much on marketing.

"We never would have guessed that Covid would bring something so great for our business," she says. Now she's at Wouldn't Go Back. This change, once forced upon her, is now something she's carrying into the future.

But of course, we cannot rely on moments of crisis to push us forward. That's a crazy way to live. (Just look at government: There's rarely a will to act until something is broken, which is why things are always breaking.) Instead, crisis should teach us to become more proactive. Once we discover that forced change can produce good things, we should want to replicate that on our own terms. We should, in theory, feel freer to make change at any time! But . . . we don't. After a moment of instability, we settle into new routines and new comforts. A breakup leads to a new relationship. Getting fired leads to getting hired. We discover a new opportunity, and then cling to it just as hard as we clung to the previous one, and we often don't adapt or adjust or revise along the way. We forget the lesson we learned about change—which all but ensures we'll have to learn it again.

As a parent, I often marvel at how this plays out in the smallest, most ridiculous, most fundamental ways. For example, there was my son's reaction to new shoes. Up until the age of five, he'd have a total meltdown whenever we'd buy him new shoes. He kept saying he preferred his *old* shoes. My wife and I would have to spend days and sometimes weeks cajoling him into his new shoes—and then, of course, he'd come to like the new shoes and we'd be able to throw the old shoes out. Then the cycle would repeat itself in a few months, when he would outgrow the new shoes (or they would fall apart or become too smelly). Because by then, of course, the new shoes had become the old shoes. "You used to hate the shoes you now love," I'd always tell him. "That means you'll love these shoes you now hate."

It never worked. Logic is no force against emotion.

So how do we break this cycle for ourselves? Tactics and strategies can help, sure, but it really must begin with the belief that nothing can—or should—be permanent.

Adam Singolda's story captures this well. He's the founder and CEO of Taboola, a company whose name you may not know, but whose products you are familiar with. At the bottom of many news websites, you'll find links to articles with pointed headlines that you cannot ignore like, "15 Foods You Should Never Eat After Age 30," which might leave you to wonder, *Am I eating those foods?!* This is an advertisement that Taboola calls "content discovery." When you click, you're taken to another site to read the story. Taboola is the largest such company that facilitates these kinds of ads, and it drives more than $1 billion in revenue each year. But back in 2019, Singolda came close to radically growing his company even more—and then it all fell apart.

In 2019, Singolda helped engineer a merger between Taboola and its biggest competitor, Outbrain. I spoke with Singolda after the announcement, and he was giddy and full of energy. We talked about his large-scale plans, and how he'd navigated the deal and secured the CEO role for himself. He detailed how he'd flown to Israel, where Outbrain has a global office (and where Singolda grew up), and how he addressed the team there while wearing a Voltron shirt. Any child of the eighties would appreciate the symbolism: In Voltron, multiple robots form together into an evil-fighting super-robot, just as these two companies were now joining forces. "I couldn't believe that moment," Singolda said. "It was surreal."

Less than a year later, the merger was called off—destroyed by a bunch of complex financial reasons. I caught up with Singolda afterward and asked how he felt. He'd been preparing to lead this much larger company, and I wondered if his original role as Taboola's leader now felt unsatisfying.

But he surprised me with his answer. Yes, sure, it was hard to lose the merger, he said. A lot of thought and energy went into calling it off. But he put the experience into context. "You have to really believe in your journey," he said, "and you have to really work hard for your luck." He told me about his management team, which has been with him for almost ten years. Together, they've gone through many ups and downs: There were the times nobody wanted to invest in Taboola, and when sales cycles slowed, and the two or three times they nearly shut the company down. "I've seen bad stuff," Singolda said. "If you're doing things for the journey, and you have people around you that make you feel invincible, then any loss is just a moment in time. It doesn't define you."

He said he thought about Netflix's early days, when it tried to sell itself to Blockbuster for $50 million. Blockbuster turned the deal down. "I can only imagine [Netflix co-chief executive] Reed Hastings calling his wife and telling her, like, 'I failed. I pitched Netflix for $50 million and it didn't work.'" Had Hastings seen that moment as the end of his journey, it would have indeed been a failure. But now we know more of the story: Netflix is a public company worth more than $200 billion. The Blockbuster deal was just a blip along the way.

Singolda has a lot more story to write, too, and it's why he's able to shake off unexpected changes. He's thinking long-term—and in 2021, a few months after we spoke, he took the company public.

This is the holistic perspective we need if we want to adapt to change. We must accept that even gigantic, life-changing shifts are just a *part* of our journey, and perhaps even an advantageous part. Singolda, like most people, was not born with this instinct. He honed it through a dozen-plus years of running Taboola, and repeatedly surviving disaster. We all must go through our own version of that process—first of understanding why we react to change the way that we do, and then laying out a plan to feel more resilient, acting more adaptable, and finally seizing the massive opportunities ahead.

That's what we're going to do in this book.

Four Phases to Change

The book is organized around the four phases of change that I gleaned from interviewing successful entrepreneurs, and that it seems we are collectively experiencing while grappling with tectonic shifts in work, culture, and life. Each section contains lessons from history and lessons from today's great changemakers. Additionally, there are plenty of actionable steps you can take to become more resilient, and ultimately more successful. The four sections are:

Part 1: Panic

This is where we explore why change is terrifying. We'll look back at moments in history when everyone opposed the things we love today, as well as today's fears of things we'll love tomorrow. Through this, we can learn a lot about how we react to change—and what instincts we must combat.

Part 2: Adaptation

Change is coming. Sometimes we see it approaching in the distance; sometimes it springs up on us suddenly. What do we do during these times? How do we know when change is worthwhile? In this section, we examine our own relationship with change—and how to feel more grounded.

Part 3: New Normal

Change has arrived. We now accept that it is unavoidable and inescapable. We may feel like our lives are displaced, but we also must build something new for ourselves. Where do we begin?

Part 4: Wouldn't Go Back

This is our destination. We'll explore how to reach that Wouldn't Go Back moment, by finding something so powerfully new that you'll be thankful for the process.

We may not be able to predict what's coming, but there is work we can do now. We can begin to build a trust inside ourselves, to feel confidence that we *can* make the most of the future. Change will always be part of the bargain. We only do ourselves harm by clinging to the past, and by believing that yesterday contained all the answers. It doesn't. We must build, and there is only one direction to build in. It is toward tomorrow.

PART 1

Panic

You know the feeling.

Change comes and we feel powerless. It's like fighting an invisible army in the darkness. Where do we even begin? What is even the problem? We don't feel like we have the time to truly understand the situation, and so all we want to do is *make it stop.* Then we make one of two irrational decisions: We either go into a defensive crouch and do absolutely nothing, or we make a rash decision that we hope will solve everything.

Neither option tends to work out well.

In this first section of the book, we'll explore where the panic comes from and how to calm it. But first, let's look at how panic can compound into gigantic mistakes—and the result, in one case, was pink margarine.

In the mid-1800s, the French emperor Napoleon III wanted a butter-like substance that could travel easily with his soldiers. He offered an award to anyone who could make it, and in 1869, a chemist named Hippolyte Mège-Mouriès cashed in. He created a concoction out of beef tallow that spread like butter and he named it oleomargarine. Soon this new food—first called oleo, later called margarine—traveled across the Atlantic, where it became a lifeline for many Americans.

"If you're thinking about the early-nineteenth-century working-class person, what they had to eat was a crust of stale bread," says Megan Elias, the director of the gastronomy program at Boston University. "And putting some kind of fat on that not only made it go down a little easier, but it also gave them nutrients that they weren't getting otherwise." These people may have preferred butter, but that was rarely an option. Butter was prohibitively expensive then, and, because this was an era before refrigeration, there was no way to store it for long anyway. Margarine, on the other hand, was cheap and fatty. It was valuable.

The butter industry saw this and panicked. In 1874, the industry declared that every measure must be taken to ensure "supremacy of the dairy in our agriculture"—and so, they hit the streets. They started fear campaigns, trying to convince people that margarine was unsafe. By the mid-1880s, they'd helped seventeen states pass some kind of law to regulate margarine, and seven states had outright banned its manufacture and sale. In 1886, Congress passed the Oleomargarine Act, which made the stuff far more expensive to produce and sell. Lobbyists then convinced many states to mandate that margarine be dyed an unappealing color—usually pink or black, but also red and brown—so that it would look unappetizing.

Now, maybe you say: *That's not panic; that's just fierce competition!* But I disagree. The butter industry could have stepped back and explored *why* people preferred this cheap butter-like substance. It could have taken steps to make its own product cheaper and more accessible, thereby expanding its marketplace. Hell, refrigeration technology was right around the corner—an innovative butter executive could have pioneered this new cooling process and been a hero to all. But instead, Big Butter saw change and wanted to stop it. That's panic.

As a result, butter producers slowed down margarine sales . . . for a little. In 1898, the Supreme Court said that states *couldn't* actually mandate that margarine be dyed strange colors—but states *could* stop margarine from being sold as yellow. From then on, margarine was often sold as white. This helped margarine develop an air of exoticness, which made consumers want it more. People would sneak it across state borders, into places where its sale was banned. And margarine companies found a clever workaround to the coloring laws: They included a packet of food coloring in the jar, so consumers could mix the yellow in themselves, which kids loved. "You had a generation growing up with the idea that *butter* was this white thing that you mixed yellow color into," says butter historian Elaine Khosrova. By the 1950s, the tables fully turned: Butter became the subject of health scares, and Americans went on to consume more margarine than butter for five decades.

Butter ultimately made a comeback. But today, dairy producers are in a similar panic about the growth of nondairy "milks" like oat milk and almond milk. As a result, they're following the same panic playbook: Instead of innovating, they're pushing laws that limit the use of words like *milk*. The result will be predictable. When someone tries to *stop* a change, rather than tries to understand the source of that change, they'll only hurt themselves in the long run.

Panic is not something to harness, and it is not something to hide from. Panic is something to overcome.

Let's start.

chapter 1

You Come from the Future

Jesse Kirshbaum's clients have been in a panic.

This is understandable. They're musicians, and popular musicians once had relatively straightforward careers: They scored recording contracts, sold their music to fans, maybe also sold it to advertising and television producers, and they toured and hawked swag. As a longtime music agent, Kirshbaum has been in the business of making this business happen. The company he founded, Nue Agency, works with some of the biggest names in entertainment. But the industry's old tricks are stumbling. Streaming services have decimated CD sales. Record labels aren't what they once were. As a result, many musicians are furious at the likes of Spotify. And now it's Kirshbaum's job to figure out how to fix this mess and make his clients money.

"If you think that change is opportunity," Kirshbaum said to me, "then what would you say to my clients?"

"Do you know who John Philip Sousa is?" I replied.

Kirshbaum did not. But he should. Sousa was once among the most famous musicians in America, and he, too, felt left behind by a massive shift in the music industry, and he, too, responded with panic. But now that we look back upon his story, we can see just how much energy he wasted.

When we feel panic, I suspect it's in part because we feel alone. We think we're experiencing something that nobody else has, and we imagine that there is no playbook for what's next. We feel like guinea pigs—and nobody wants to be the guinea pig! We want to be the Tesla driving through a beautiful, mountainous pass, long after somebody else dynamited their way through the rock and smoothly paved the road.

But here's the surprising truth that's hard to recognize at the beginning of change: Even when we feel lost, we are, without realizing it, still driving along that smoothed-out mountainous pass. Someone before us *already* dealt with what we're dealing with now. There actually *is* evidence of the path forward. All we need to do is take it seriously.

That's what really drew me to history. When I started looking backward in time, to moments when other industries were disrupted and other lives were altered, I saw a lot of the same fear and resistance that we see about today's changes. Today's fears about privacy and misinformation on the internet? They were expressed in the 1800s about the telegraph. Today's parental guilt over kids' addiction to screens? You'll find 1920s parents bemoaning radio in the same way. With the benefit of hindsight, we can see how panic never led us to solutions—but it *did* inhibit people from maximizing their lives. They were so focused on losing the old opportunities, they failed to see new ones.

This helped me coalesce around a theory about change. I call it: You Come from the Future.

As we begin to untangle the panic around change, I want to prove to you that you come from the future. It is a liberating realization. And it all starts with John Philip Sousa.

The Drumbeat of Panic

You, too, may not know much about Sousa. But you do know his music.

Sousa was born in 1854, in an era where all music was performed live. There was no radio when he was born, nor were record players available. If you wanted to hear music then, musicians would need to pick up their instruments and play for you in a one-time, unrecorded, never-to-be-heard-again performance. This is how it had always been.

Sousa learned the violin at an early age. At age thirteen, he joined the United States Marine Band. He also studied music privately and learned not just to perform but to compose and to conduct large orchestras. He composed what would become some of the most famous marches in American history. His song "The Stars and Stripes Forever" was designated the national march of the United States of America and his "Semper Fidelis" became the official march of the United States Marine Corps. When a fledgling newspaper called *The Washington Post* hired him to write a march, he wrote "The Washington Post," which is still performed regularly today.

All of this made Sousa very famous—one of the biggest names in music at the time. He was a household name who'd pack concert halls, where his music gave warmth and soul to a nation still healing from the Civil War, and where it would eventually rouse them to patriotic duty during World War I.

But his era was coming to a close. In the early 1900s, two things changed. The first big change was the phonograph, an early version of the record player. With this device, for the very first time in human history, music could be recorded and replayed. Time could be captured. No concert hall was required to hear a concert.

This worried a lot of people. Today we're concerned that social media frays our social connections, or that artificial intelligence is a dangerous replacement for human work—and back then, in the early 1900s, those same concerns were applied to the phonograph. "Does not frequent use of the phonograph, especially in continual repetitions of a number, produce inattention in the hearer?" asked *The Brooklyn Daily Eagle,* echoing many worries of the time. "The music is so easily obtainable by the listener, who sits back and is fed with sweet sounds."

Next, radio was invented. It broadcast voices and music into people's homes, which was a completely foreign concept at the time. From the very beginning of civilization, up until the invention of radio, your home was a barrier between you and the world. Nothing from outside was coming in unless you opened your door and welcomed it. Radio changed that.

This terrified Sousa, who made it his mission to destroy these new technologies. He made frequent proclamations about the shortcomings of recorded music, encouraged musicians not to participate, and wrote articles about the dangers it posed to humanity. The way he saw it, this time of change was a threat to our minds and our families. My favorite argument of his was published in *Appleton's Magazine* in 1906, where he wrote: "When a mother can turn on the phonograph with the same ease that she applies to the electric light, will she croon her baby to slumber with sweet lullabys, or will the infant be put to sleep by machinery? Children are naturally imitative, and if, in their infancy, they hear only phonographs, will they not sing, if they sing at all, in imitation, and finally become simply human phonographs—without soul or expression?"

In other words, he believed that technology would replace all forms of performance—which means that mothers would stop singing to their children, the children would instead grow up to imitate machines, and therefore we'd raise a generation of machine babies.

And the panic didn't stop there.

You've surely heard the phrase *live music.* It's common today—on the billboards of concert halls, on flyers at coffee shops, on Ticketmaster's website. But the phrase was born out of the same resistance that Sousa had led.

As recorded music technology improved, Sousa wasn't the only musician who felt threatened. Their careers were suddenly subject to change. Radio stations used to only broadcast live performances—the musicians were literally inside the studio, playing *live* for the listeners at home. Movie theaters likewise used *live* musicians; they'd perform the score of a movie in person, as people watched the screen. But soon, radio stations were playing records and movie theaters were playing soundtracks. Due to a lack of work in the late 1920s, many musicians fell into poverty.

That's when musicians tried to change the tune. "The whole term *live music* was actually introduced by the musicians union as a rhetorical attempt to oppose 'live' versus 'dead,'" said Mark Katz, a professor of music at the University of North Carolina at Chapel Hill. "They wanted consumers to think of recordings as dead, and them as alive—and who would choose death over life?" In 1928, Joseph W. Weber, the president of the American Federation of Musicians, framed the change as an existential threat to everyone. Musical machines in theaters, Weber wrote, "constitute a serious menace to cultural growth." In the 1940s, musicians went on strike twice: No union musicians would go into a studio to record anything.

"So here's why I'm telling you this," I said to Kirchbaum, the music agent, after walking through this history. "Your musicians today are worried about losing the thing that a previous generation of musicians tried to stop."

Sousa and his peers saw recorded music as an existential threat, but they were wrong. This technology was a musician's best friend. It enabled musicians to scale their work; a musician couldn't perform in every corner of the globe, but they *could* sell records (and later stream music) anywhere. With recorded music, a musician could literally make money in their sleep. Sousa himself eventually figured this out. In truth, it seems, a lot of Sousa's resistance might have been rooted in his own financial fears. People bought a lot of sheet music back then, and that made Sousa a lot of money. This new technology seemed to threaten those sales. "Then he realized he could make a lot of money from the recordings," Katz said. "So although in 1906 he railed against the phonograph, in the 1920s he praised it because suddenly he was making a lot of money off recordings. Perhaps he loosened up because his fears weren't realized, or perhaps he saw that he could make money off this thing that at first seemed a threat."

Then a lot of other people started making money, too. Recorded music technology also birthed a new generation of music-related jobs that previously didn't exist—studio musicians, audio engineers, studio managers, radio promoters, DJs, manufacturers of recording equipment and software, and more. Did some musicians lose their jobs in this transition? Yes. But they were replaced with a variety of jobs for a far wider range of people.

This evolved into a robust music industry. Records gave way to tapes, which gave way to CDs, which peaked in the year 2000 with more than 900 million discs shipped. Then CDs gave way to iTunes sales, which gave way to Spotify and other streaming services, which is where we are now, but surely is not where we'll stop. Musicians are angry about all this change, and that's understandable. An album release doesn't mean what it used to anymore, and it's much harder to make money on streams alone.

But nothing can be counted on forever, and that includes the things that feel foundational and unquestionable. Record sales weren't some natural order of the world, woven into our DNA. They were a blip— a brief moment in time, squeezed in between the decline of Sousa and the rise of Spotify. In the grand history of musicians earning a living off of music, the storage and sale of a physical object that contained a limited amount of music was an *abnormality*. It was a weird little thing that worked pretty well during a particular moment in time.

This is all we ever have, really. Everything we're comfortable with, everything we're familiar with, everything we think is proper and correct and natural—it was all a weird little thing that worked pretty well during a particular moment in time.

And that is *it*.

This is our history: It is us defending weird little things over and over again. The ice industry began with people literally chopping ice out of lakes in the winter and then storing it for summertime sales—and then those people demonized the new refrigeration industry, once machines were able to make ice all year round. They simply couldn't envision how refrigeration would revolutionize the food industry, giving many more people the opportunity to work in it. The movie industry vehemently opposed the VCR, thinking it would destroy movie theater attendance. Instead, it birthed a vital new source of revenue for movie studios. Examples like this are endless. People opposed mirrors. (They make people too vain!) People opposed pencil erasers. (Kids will become careless with their handwriting!) People even opposed watches. (Too addictive!)

Now look at us today. We are the product of all these changes. The clothing we wear, the lifestyles we choose, the music we listen to, the technology we use, the places we go, the words we use—all of this was once new, and therefore scary, and therefore opposed by a previous generation. All of it represented change. All of it was considered *bad*.

But do we think we're bad? Of course not! We think we're good. We're made up of all the good things—the familiar, comfortable, necessary things. The things we grew up with. The things we understand. Then when change comes to us, we instinctively recoil. We say, "No! You can't change this! These are all the good things!"

In short, we repeat the mistakes of the past.

You want to see what change actually looks like? Look at yourself. *You come from the future.* You are the product of that change! Now follow the logic of that. If you think you're good, then you are the living evidence that change can be good. This means that the next wave of change is not inherently bad. If it is not inherently bad, then it must present a range of opportunities. And you have the ability to participate in and help shape those opportunities right now.

This should be liberating, because once we accept how true this is, we can use it as our guide through another truism of the future. It goes like this: *The future is not optional.*

Change is coming. It's here. It cannot be stopped! And when it comes for us, we really only have two choices—to embrace it, or to fight a losing fight.

So that's what I said to Kirshbaum, the music agent. Do not panic. Do not focus on what is lost. Focus instead on what can be gained, so you can get there first. And a year after we spoke, he did exactly that: He handed off his agency's day-to-day business, stepped into a partner role, and then took a job as CMO of a startup called Dreamstage, which aims to reinvent the virtual concert business. "I wanted to be better positioned for where I think the industry is going," he said.

And *how* do you better position yourself for where things are going? We'll get there later in the book. First, let's investigate exactly how our panic can impact us. Because while panic is not productive, the results of panic are definitely instructive.

chapter 2

Why We Keep Panicking

Do you remember Facebook Depression?

It was all anyone could talk about in 2011. Twitter was obscure and confusing, Instagram was just one of many little photo-sharing apps, and Snapchat and TikTok didn't exist. Nobody could imagine Facebook ultimately becoming a force in politics; it was simply the website that hoovered up people's time and memories. More than a million photos were typically uploaded every day back then—and more than 750 million photos were uploaded on New Year's Eve weekend alone. But then the news got dark. Researchers began connecting Facebook use to a decline in mental health, and that made headlines around the world.

"As if being a teenager wasn't hard enough," said the news anchor of ABC Action News in Tampa Bay, Florida, "doctors are now warning teens: Their Facebook obsession could lead to depression."

"'Facebook Depression' Seen as New Risk for Teens," shouted a CBS News headline. "Pediatricians Should Discuss 'Facebook Depression' with Kids," urged *Time* magazine.

All this news was generated by a single event: In 2011, the American Academy of Pediatrics had published a paper called "The Impact of Social Media on Children, Adolescents, and Families." It warned doctors about a new phenomenon it called "Facebook Depression," which it defined as a "depression that develops when preteens and teens spend a great deal of time on social media sites, such as Facebook, and then begin to exhibit classic symptoms of depression."

This understandably freaked parents out. Were their children being harmed by this strange new form of socializing?

The answer would take years to be revealed. But now we have it, and it's very different from the public narrative: Although individual people of course can have bad experiences online, no research has proven that normal exposure to social media harms adolescent psychological well-being. But when parents act rashly out of concern for things like Facebook Depression, they may inadvertently be the ones causing harm themselves. (I'll explain why soon.)

In this way, Facebook Depression serves as an important object lesson for how change can be misinterpreted. When our default position is to panic, we become impatient for solutions, do not consider all the information available, and make counterproductive decisions. This is as true on a societal level as it is on an individual level.

If we are to guard ourselves against future panics, then it's helpful to understanding where a problem like this comes from. Let's start with the researcher who has seen this particular issue up close. Her name is Amy Orben.

Panic vs. Data

Amy Orben wanted to answer a very modern question: How do digital connections compare with other forms of connection?

It's the kind of thing only a wonky, hyperanalytic person would think to ask. Orben is that person. She received a master's in natural science from the University of Cambridge, and then went to the University of Oxford for a doctorate in experimental psychology (where she was also nominated for a "Best Tutor" award by Oxford Student Union, because of course). This is a woman who knows how to quantify the world around her and then navigate the numbers. For her thesis, she'd become curious about how social connections change over time—and to figure that out, she needed to literally measure the value of different social connections. Could you somehow quantify the value of a hug? Is it worth, I don't know . . . *ten human points*? And if that was possible, could you do the same for receiving an email, or sending a voice memo, or talking by Face-Time? Then could you compare the two? Seven emails plus 1.75 voice memos plus 23.6 FaceTime minutes equals a minute-long hug?

I'm simplifying the idea here, but it doesn't matter: Ultimately, these calculations weren't possible. The data didn't exist. So she had to shift. She needed a compelling thesis project related to how digital technologies impact social connections. This was 2017, and the world was still having a big panic about social media's impact on young people's mental health. Orben thought this was the perfect opportunity. She could investigate these big, important subjects that were grabbing headlines around the world, and hopefully come away with insights that could help improve lives. "It felt so urgent," she told me. "It felt like every minute mattered."

For the next few years, this is what she devoted her attention to. Eventually she thought it would be fun to kick her paper off with a historical anecdote—something that contextualized the danger of social media. She went to the library and came across a 1941 article in *The Journal of Pediatrics,* which warned about the dangers of radio. "The average child radio addict starts lapping up his fascinating crime at about 4 o'clock in the afternoon and continues for much of the time until sent to bed," wrote the author, a doctor named Mary Preston. "The spoiled children listen until around 10 o'clock; the less indulged until around 9 o'clock."

The report concluded that more than half of children had become addicted to radio dramas.

Orben was stunned. "It felt like it was exactly the same conversation I've been having for three years—just, you know, eighty years before," she said. This led her to ask herself some very large and existential questions like: *Is any of this real? And is this what I want to do for the next forty years of my life?*

She completed her thesis anyway and, before becoming a college research fellow at the University of Cambridge, she continued her research at Oxford. But she hadn't recovered from that shock at the library. She'd been investigating how social media impacts children's mental health, thinking it was an original question about modern technological change. Now she knew it was actually an *unoriginal* question that's posed about *any* technological change. Was she just part of a cycle that repeated itself over and over? Orben started looking back at her research—and all the other studies she'd found about social media—but now with this new lens. She re-analyzed the data from past studies—studies that had gotten a lot of attention over the years, and that had been used as the foundation for many books and articles and political hand-wringing. The results were alarmingly clear.

"The research was flawed," she said. "They didn't really tell us a lot about whether there's a causal impact of social media on depression. We're all talking about *correlations*—and they're very, very small." It was a classic data analysis problem: Are we looking at causation or correlation? Did X cause Y, or is X simply happening at the same time as Y? A dog urinates on a tree, and the tree falls down the next day. Did the dog do that?

To understand how so many researchers got it wrong, let's dig into the data. Most of those old studies were based on analyses of large, publicly available data sets—and Orben said they are rife with problems. First, the data is generally self-reported: Teens were simply answering questions like, "How much do you use social media on a normal weekday?" and "How are you feeling?" This will solicit very imperfect answers. (I mean, do *you* know exactly how long you spent looking at Instagram last Tuesday, and how it made you feel relative to anything else going on in your life that day?)* Second, the data is susceptible to researcher bias. To prove the point, in a paper that Orben and a coauthor published about this in the journal *Nature Human Behavior* in 2019, they found 600 million different conclusions that could be drawn from the data sets. If a researcher was inclined to see a connection between social media use and mental health decline, they had many potential conclusions to choose from.

So how do you visualize and understand researcher bias? You use what's called a Specification Curve Analysis—which, to oversimplify, means looking at the data in many ways and then evaluating the results across all of the results. *Scientific American* describes it as "the statistical equivalent of seeing the forest for the trees." This is what Orben and her colleagues did for all the available data on more than 350,000 adolescents, and this helped them take into account other factors that impact a young person's mental health. "The connection between things like well-being and technology are inherently complicated," Orben said, "We often think of them as a one-way street—you know, technology affects

---

* This self-reporting problem also plagued an internal Facebook report, which became a big story in 2021 after *The Wall Street Journal* revealed it. When Facebook surveyed people about how Instagram made them feel, three out of ten girls said the app made them feel worse about themselves. "But such a finding should be used as a starting point for research, not as a conclusion," cautioned Laurence Steinberg, a professor of psychology at Temple University and an expert on adolescence, in a column he wrote in *The New York Times*. "Psychological research has repeatedly shown that we often don't understand ourselves as well as we think we do."

us. But actually, the way we feel also impacts the way we use technologies. And other third factors, especially for children and teenagers—like their backgrounds, their parents, their motivations—those all impact this very complicated network."

After running the numbers on this deeper and more sophisticated analysis, Orben uncovered a very different reality from the alarming studies she'd been reviewing. In actuality, technology alone has an *insubstantial* effect on young people's psychological well-being. Orben, a great lover of data, was able to compare how different activities relate to well-being, as a way to understand whether social media is really having a large and important impact. *Scientific American* succinctly summed up her results: "Technology use tilts the needle less than half a percent away from feeling emotionally sound. For context, eating potatoes is associated with nearly the same degree of effect and wearing glasses has a more negative impact on adolescent mental health."

Eating potatoes! Oh, the irony: When the potato spread through Europe in the 1500s, it was sometimes called "the devil's apple" and accused of being used by witches. People were skeptical because, among other reasons, the potato never appears in the Bible. Now here we are, many centuries later, and our attitude about potatoes has improved . . . but our attitudes about social media are evolving. It turns out they have roughly the same (negligible) impact on young minds.

Many other studies have since reached similar conclusions. Soon Orben got to wondering: Why did this misunderstanding happen at all? In theory, we had already learned this lesson back in the 1940s—when research warned of radio's harmful effects on children, and then radio-listening children grew up to be just fine. Why didn't the lesson stick?

In answering that question, she came up with a four-step theory she calls the Sisyphean Cycle of Technology Panics. It can tell us a lot—not just about how we react to technology, but about how we react to new things in general. Facebook Depression is simply Exhibit A.

Your Place in the Sisyphean Cycle

Sisyphus: He's the guy from Greek mythology who was doomed to roll a boulder up a hill, only to have the boulder roll back down, and then have to do it repeatedly for eternity. You can see why this makes for a tidy metaphor.

As Orben studied the history of technology-fueled panics, she came to see a very similar cycle. We, as a society, would grow fearful of something new, and then launch a long and painful process that often ended unproductively. Then we'd do the whole thing over again with another new technology, as if the previous cycle never happened.

After studying this for about a year, Orben was able to break down exactly what is happening, and in what order. While the process she identified is driven by large systems and populations, it's not hard to see how this can apply to any one individual, in any moment of change. We'll eventually zoom in on the personal level—but first, here are the four stages she identified.

Step 1: Something seems different

A new technology is introduced, and its adoption starts to change the behavior of people seen as vulnerable, like children. Then that change becomes linked to whatever large, abstract concern is already floating around in society. For example, in the 1950s, kids became obsessed with a game called pinball, and that meant their habits changed. They were inside more, rather than running around outside. Adults started gambling on pinball, so it was assumed that children gambled, too. This then got lumped in with the broader 1950s moral panic over juvenile delinquency—a belief that young people were becoming more violent and anti-establishment. Pinball then became identified as one of the causes of this delinquency.

Why do we make that leap? Orben attributes it to a thinking called "technological determinism." This isn't new; Karl Marx wrote a lot about it. It goes like this: Instead of looking at the world as a complex series of slow-moving social and economic factors, we tend to see it as being impacted most by whatever's newest and loudest. We believe that our technologies are the primary things that shape our society—and when the technologies change, we change as a result. "We feel like technologies affect us," Orben said, "but we cannot affect them."

The concern begins at a grassroots level; at first it's just adults talking among themselves. Then it gets picked up and amplified by the media, which is interested in what people are worried about. Then . . .

Step 2: Politicians get involved

Politicians love a good moral panic, because they make complex problems appear simple. Is there a rise of juvenile delinquency? Nobody wants to address the structural inequality that may be causing it—that requires blaming voters, and examining a politicians' own policies, and then making difficult and lasting change. Instead, politicians are much happier to just dump the blame on a pinball manufacturer. It's easier and swiftly translates to glowing media attention.

This is how, for example, we got New York City mayor Fiorello La Guardia smashing pinball machines with a sledgehammer and throwing them into the river, as news cameras watched. That really happened. Then mayors across America started banning pinball machines; police literally went door to door seeking out the forbidden game.

But politicians don't just act—they also seek *evidence* to justify their actions. And this is where it gets really interesting.

Step 3: Scientists hit the gas

Centuries ago, when people wanted to know how to think or handle a difficult question, they sought guidance from the leaders they trusted most—chieftains, elders, priests. Now, Orben said, they increasingly seek it from scientists. "How to raise your child, for example, wasn't a question for science for a really, really long time," she said. "It was more of a question of family, religious, or community traditions."

This shift is good in many respects. Science reveals important answers and helps us evolve our understanding of everything from diet to child-rearing to why we should all have standing desks. But there are hiccups. First, people often confuse *data* with *application.* Just because science identifies trends in data, that doesn't mean researchers know how to apply it to real people. (Orben, for example, receives regular calls from journalists who are asking her parenting advice—which she feels extremely unqualified to give.) But even more important, for as much as society at large now turns to science for answers, society at large also doesn't really understand the scientific process.

Second, there's a question of money. Science relies heavily upon grants. Grants rely upon sources of funding. And funding often relies upon whatever donors and policy makers think is interesting and important. This is why Congress will sometimes debate which organizations get scientific funding, or why politicians will feign outrage over a silly study they don't like. It's a way to signal their values and priorities to voters. And according to Orben, it has very real consequences over what kind of science gets done, because researchers begin lining up to study whichever subjects are in favor. "It's interesting and helps our careers if we research something people actually care about," she said.

But good science takes time. It is not about individual results; it is about consensus. Good science means looking at a data set, drawing a conclusion, publishing it, and then waiting for other scientists to look at those results and say, "Hmmm, I dunno about that." Then they do their own research. This is what happened when Orben discovered the many errors in prior social media research. It wasn't a flaw in science; it's how the process is supposed to work.

Politicians do not have time for that, though. They want answers *now*. So researchers try to speed up their work. They tweet and talk to journalists and design studies that can move quickly. And that leads to . . .

Step 4: The low-information free-for-all

Once researchers release the results of their time-consuming studies, the media reports on them. Then politicians start acting on them. And then there's chaos.

What does that look like? Well, imagine that you're an ambitious senator named Estes Kefauver in the 1950s. Your constituents are worried about juvenile delinquency, and you're positioning yourself for a run for president, so you hype a Senate investigation into the harmful effects of something even more insidious than pinball—and that is comic books. As your star witness at this hearing, you call . . . a *scientist*! It's a psychologist named Fredric Wertham, who has done a seemingly scientific review of the problem, and who now sits in front of a U.S. Senate subcommittee and says, "It is my opinion without any reasonable doubt and without any reservation that comic books are an important contributing factor in many cases of juvenile delinquency."

Never mind that Wertham's work would eventually be revealed to be full of holes and total fabrications, or that future studies would find massive benefits to reading comic books—from improved literacy to fostering children's healthy imaginations. That review process was too slow. Wertham beat everyone to the punch, so his research controlled the narrative.

And what is the final result of this Sisyphean Cycle—the four steps of fear, bubbling up through politics and science? According to Orben, it's mostly a lot of fuss. Policy makers make noise, very little is achieved, and then something else comes along and the entire system repeats itself. "Quite quickly, the conversation dies down," she said. "There's no more funding. There's no more interest. Scientists don't get their media interviews. Policy makers don't have the pressure to do something anymore." Sisyphus's boulder rolls down the hill, only to be rolled up again soon enough.

But while little is ultimately accomplished, harm has been done in the process. After Wertham's testimony at the U.S. Senate, the comic book industry realized it was in trouble. To make senators happy, it created a self-censorship agency—a body called the Comics Code Authority, which ruined countless artists' careers and flattened the industry's creativity and growth for decades.

In the case of Facebook Depression, it received international attention in 2011, after a scientific report found a connection between teenagers' depression and Facebook use. Although Orben's research didn't specifically examine Facebook Depression, her work revealed how tenuous a connection like that was: As it turns out, there is a tiny *correlation*—not a causation!—between Facebook use and depression among teenagers. And again, no other study has ever proven a causation. The most important question now is: What is the result of this panic?

Here's one. According to the logic of Facebook Depression, the social media network was causing the depression. If that's the case, then parents might reasonably take Facebook away from their children. But now we know that Facebook use isn't a large predictor of well-being. What if, instead, depressed teenagers simply tended to be more frequent users of Facebook, maybe because they found a community there? So if parents took Facebook away from their kids, based on a misunderstanding of the situation, they'd have severed these children from a valuable community, and so the solution actually *caused more problems.*

Are there real problems with social media? Of course there are. New things disrupt old things; some new habits are healthier than others. We should always be alert, and always have conversations about the best ways to make life better for everyone. We should promote responsible usage. But when we default to panic, and then move so fast that we don't gain an accurate understanding of change, we are not able to properly identify a problem. If we can't do that, we sure as hell can't properly create solutions. This is the danger of the Sisyphean Cycle.

But are we actually doomed to repeat it, over and over, like Sisyphus himself? Maybe not.

How to Break the Cycle

I asked Orben if there is a way out of this.

Yes, she said, there might be—but it means that science must play a different role in the cycle. Instead of being reactive, science should be proactive. If researchers need multiple years to truly begin understanding something, then that long-term process shouldn't start while everyone's all hyped up and politicians are demanding answers. It should start *before anyone cares.*

"If we know that a new panic is coming in maybe five or ten years," Orben told me, "then what we should be doing now is putting our feelers out, and trying to figure out what that might be, and start collecting data."

This is a wise answer that goes beyond just science. Orben isn't saying that her peers must do better. She's instead saying that her peers must recognize their weaknesses. In effect, she's saying that she believes in the scientific process—but that, because it is slow and messy, the people who participate in it should factor those downsides into their work. If you need an answer today, and your process takes five years, then you don't start today. You start five years ago.

We can and should apply this to ourselves as well. We need a situational awareness of ourselves—a recognition of how we, as individuals and as groups, react negatively to new things. What did we once fear, that we now love? What did we learn in the process? Then we can build that knowledge into our actions.

When I was a kid, for example, my parents forced me to go to summer camp. I screamed at them for it. I told them I'd have a terrible time. What did I really want instead? I wanted to sit at home all summer watching TV with my friends. But my parents shipped me off anyway, onward to a new experience I didn't want—and I ended up loving it. The lesson for me, which I took a long time to learn, was this: *When I'm asked to do something new, I will imagine all the reasons I'll hate it . . . but I might actually enjoy it. So the most important thing for me to do is: Don't say no.*

Tariq Farid also learned this lesson after resisting something new, though the stakes were considerably higher. He's the founder of Edible Arrangements, an international franchise company that made its name selling pieces of fruit that are speared on sticks and arranged like they're flower bouquets. The concept dates back to 1997, when he owned a few flower shops in Connecticut and came up with this idea for arrangements people could eat. At first he called them Delicious Designs, but someone suggested the catchier name Edible Arrangements, and so he went with it—initially just using the name for his product, and then for his company, and then, in 2013, he shortened his company's name to simply Edibles. After decades in the business, Farid felt an ownership over that word.

Then the legal cannabis movement came along.

In 2016, California passed what was called Proposition 64, which legalized recreational marijuana in many forms—including "edibles." The word was right there in the bill, familiar to any pot lover who has long used the word to describe a brownie, gummy, or any other food-like product infused with cannabis. Farid had no idea about this; he's not a marijuana user. But once he saw the word—his word!—in the California bill, he entered a full-on phase one Panic. "We have to do something about this," he said to himself. He felt like his life's work was on the line.

Farid called his lawyer. They drew up a lobbying plan. He readied himself for a big, expensive fight. The goal was to stop lawmakers and everyone else from using the word *edible* to refer to . . . well, edibles as millions of people knew them. Farid spent about a year fighting this hopeless battle, until finally, during one lobbying trip, someone told him there were two ways to look at his situation: "You can look at it as a tsunami—and if it's a tsunami, get out of the way," the person told him. "Or you can look at it as a really nice wave—and go get your surfboard out."

This made Farid stop and reflect. Did he really understand the situation he was in? Was this a destructive tsunami, or was it a wave he could ride? He did not know. So he decided to get a more clear-eyed view. He immersed himself in cannabis literature. He subscribed to industry magazines and started visiting cannabis production facilities. He discovered that, yes, while people used cannabis to get high, there was an adjacent world of cannabis-derived CBD products that did not alter anyone's mind, and that was popular in the wellness industry. Farid heard that CBD is popular with moms, and he lit up. "For me, that word, *mom,* was like—oh!" Farid says.

He decided he needed to change strategies. Instead of spending money on lawyers to fight a tsunami, he needed to invest in a surfboard. So he did, in the form of buying forty acres of hemp that he used to develop his company's first-ever CBD powder. He then opened a retail store in Connecticut called Incredible Edibles, to sell CBD products. This hasn't exactly transformed his business, but it's given Farid a toehold in a potential new growth industry. And perhaps most important, it simply stopped Farid's Panic, which allowed him to refocus his time and resources on more important things.

I'll repeat what I wrote above, now that you've seen it in action: When we default to Panic, and then move so fast that we don't gain an accurate understanding of change, we are not able to properly identify a problem. If we can't do that, we sure as hell can't properly create solutions.

Farid never had a cannabis problem. He had a panic problem.

You have had experiences like this, too. Maybe some of them were giant learning experiences, like Farid's. Maybe some of them were small and ultimately pointless, like how I kept resisting summer camp, and we don't remember all of these examples because we tend to remember good experiences a lot longer than we remember bad ones. This means we may not recall all the resistance we kicked up! And if we forget, then we can't learn.

It's time to keep a record. The next time you surprise yourself by loving something you thought you'd hate, write it down. Memorialize it in a notebook, or on a Word doc, or just an email to yourself. Describe why you didn't want to do this thing, and then what happened after you did it, and how you feel now. Then store that piece of writing somewhere that you can easily find—because one day, I guarantee, the boulder you just rolled up a hill will roll back down, and you'll be at the bottom, feeling lazy and defeated, and you will not want to push it back up. That's when you need the reminder that you've been there before—but that there are great things on the other side of these feelings. All you need to do is say yes.

That's when you break the Sisyphean Cycle. And you can begin to focus on what's next.

chapter 3

Extrapolate the Gain

The Sisyphean Cycle does an excellent job of explaining *how* Panic blossoms, but it doesn't quite explain how the fear gets started in the first place, or why every new thing we see and experience can feel so overwhelming.

Perhaps it is *loss*.

When something new arrives, we can easily imagine all the comfortable things we'll lose—but we struggle to imagine the exciting things we gain. Then we extrapolate the loss, imagining (often without evidence) how one change will trigger even more drastic losses. This, I believe, is the number one reason why people struggle with change.

Whenever I tell people this, they tend to push back. *I can't just ignore what I'm losing,* they say. If there actually is something to gain from change, they feel like it'll be a consolation prize—a little lollipop to suck on after losing what we really wanted. So to gain some distance from our own sense of loss, and to see how misguided this way of thinking can be, let's go back to 1938 . . . when two adults watched a little girl named Claire read a book, and reacted in a way that we'd almost never do today.

"There's Claire with a book," the first adult said. "Always reading. I never saw such a child for a book."

"Didn't she want to go to the party?" the second adult replied. "I thought every child in town was there. They're going to see the picture. They are all simply wild with excitement. Isn't she well, or what?"

"You just can't separate her from a book," the first adult said. "She would rather read than do anything else. I try to get her to play with the others, but she says they are too silly, that their games are childish. They don't have any interest for her. She would rather stay home and read a good book."

"Mm-m-m," the second said. "Too bad."

This dialogue comes directly out of a 1938 story from *The St. Petersburg Times*. Its headline: "Too Much Reading Is Harmful." After telling the story of poor little Claire, it goes on to detail the many ways that novels are addictive and can stunt a young person's development. It reads as if it came out of a parallel universe—one where puppies are ugly and rainbows darken the sky. But consider the value judgments built into the dialogue: In-person group activities were considered natural, while solitary engagement with a device was viewed as isolating and harmful.

Now it sounds a little more familiar, doesn't it?

As it turns out, long before we worried about kids being consumed by video games and social media, centuries' worth of thinkers were concerned about books. Novels had been around in some form for thousands of years, but they proliferated (and therefore triggered alarms) in the late 1700s as printing technology became cheaper. In 1778, the English essayist Vicessimus Knox warned that books "often pollute the heart in the recesses of the closet, inflame the passions at a distance from temptation, and teach all the malignity of vice in solitude." American founding father Thomas Jefferson was similarly concerned; he wrote a letter in 1818 that described novels as "poison [that] infects the mind." By the late 1800s, newspapers were full of reports about brainwashed youths living a life of crime. In 1883, *The New York Times* reported on two boys who shot a cabdriver during a robbery. What made them do it? "The accused are boys addicted to dime novel reading," the article said.

What's going on here?

In 1931, novels were equated with *loss*.

Loss, like I said, is always easier to see than gain. That is our consistent problem. But fortunately, it can also be our solution.

Learning to Live with Loss

Imagine that I handed you $1,000, and then gave you two options. Which of these would you rather do?

- a. Play a game: You have a 50% chance of winning another $1,000 . . . and a 50% chance of losing it all.
- b. Don't play the game. You can keep $500, guaranteed.

Now, let's run a similar experiment. Which of these two options do you prefer?

- a. Play a game: You have a 50% chance of winning a three-week tour of England, France, and Italy . . . and a 50% chance of winning nothing.
- b. Don't play the game: You're guaranteed a one-week tour of England.

Did you pick b both times? If so, you are in the vast majority of people. If you picked a, you either have a unique way of assessing risk . . . or you're just lying. (Stop lying!)

These questions originated as part of a groundbreaking 1979 study by Daniel Kahneman and Amos Tversky, which helped shape the field of behavioral science and earned a Nobel Prize. Respondents vastly preferred to take smaller, guaranteed prizes. They rarely gambled for the bigger ones. In the case of the European tour, for example, 78% of people picked the guaranteed week in England. (Has anyone told them about the weather there?) Only 22% of people were willing to gamble for a much bigger prize.

Why don't people take the risk? Kahneman and Tversky gave it a name: "risk aversion," which is also often referred to as "loss aversion." They propose that people weigh losses more heavily than gains. Decades of science have since been built upon this idea, finding that loss aversion happens in ways big and small, and that it leads people to make decisions with little rational sense.

In one of my favorite experiments, led by psychologists at the University of Iowa, researchers broke people into groups: One group, which we'll call Build Up, was given plain pizzas and told to add as many ingredients as they want. The other group, which we'll call Scale Down, was given fully loaded pizzas and asked to remove any ingredients they didn't want. Then each group would have to "buy" the pizzas, based on whatever a pizza shop would charge for all those ingredients. The result: The Build Up group's pizzas were simple and cheap, and the Scale Down group's pizzas were loaded and expensive. What happened? In the Build Up group, people added only what they reasonably wanted. In the Scale Down group, people struggled to eliminate something that they already had. (And yes, this study was done in both America *and* Italy. Same result.)

We've all experienced some version of this. As I write this book, for example, I'm still bitter over a bet I made on Bitcoin. When an individual Bitcoin was worth $4,000, I bought two of them. Then I rode its ups and downs for a few years, until one bitcoin was worth $16,000. I assumed that was its peak, so I cashed out—and made $24,000 in profit. That felt great! But then Bitcoin kept climbing and climbing, and by the time it hit $50,000 a few months later, I wanted to plug my ears anytime someone mentioned it. I could have made $92,000! Now I just felt stupid—as if I lost money, instead of gained it.

This is hardwired into our brains. Psychologists and neuroscientists have hooked people up to brain monitors and then asked them to gamble with money. They found that brain activity was strongest in response to potential losses, and less strong in response to potential gains. Other scientists are exploring whether losses trigger more activity in the parts of the brain that process emotion—meaning we literally *feel* loss more than gain. It sticks with us longer, just like the bitter, irrational taste of my Bitcoin profit.

Of course, in all the scenarios above, people were deciding between two choices—to play or not play a game, to stack or not stack a pizza. What does all this have to do with experiencing change?

It's time to tell you the story of the scandalous umbrella.

What's So Bad About Staying Dry?

If you lived in London in the eighteenth century, you had a few options when it started raining. You could wear a long coat and just trudge through it, or if you were wealthy enough, you could hail a horse-drawn carriage. But then, on one rainy day around the year 1750, a man appeared out of the fog—and he stood upright, completely dry, while walking with some foreign object above his head. His name was Jonas Hanway, and he was the first prominent user of an umbrella in England.

People jeered. Some threw trash at him. One carriage driver tried to run Hanway over, and in turn, Hanway revealed another use for the umbrella: He hit the guy with it.

Why was everyone was so worked up?

The umbrella is at least two thousand years old, and shows up in ancient cultures around the world, including the Chinese, Egyptians, Greeks, Romans, and even the Aztecs. But even by the 1600s, it hadn't made its way to England. Then something called the Grand Tour began. It was an upscale seventeenth-century version of today's postcollegiate European backpacking trips. Young, wealthy Englishmen would travel to France, Italy, and other cultural meccas, so that they could become "cultured" in the way that European society valued. But while traveling, they learned something else, too: The rest of the world isn't as rainy as England! And when it *does* rain, people just hold a "portable roof" over their heads and keep moving.

Young Brits started bringing these umbrellas home, where they were instantly mocked. For example, in a 1709 magazine called *The Female Tatler,* "a society of ladies" wrote a piece directed at a young man they recently saw use an umbrella. If he wants to stay dry in the future, the ladies write, "he shall be welcome to the Maid's Pattens." (A translation of 1700s humor: Pattens were wooden platform overshoes worn by working-class or country women to lift their feet away from wet or dirty streets, which, it is implied, would be more dignified than carrying an umbrella.)

Obviously, much of this mockery was driven by class and snobbery—who needs a low-class umbrella if you can afford to hail a carriage? The Brits also associated umbrellas with France, which is why they derisively described umbrella users as "Frenchmen." But these were symptoms of a deeper anxiety. "What the Brits believed is that for most of their history, the rain and their insular, archipelago position, made them who they were," said Vladimir Yankovich, a senior lecturer at the University of Manchester and a historian of atmospheric sciences, when I asked him to explain all the umbrella hating. "They saw themselves as sturdy, robust, independent, and different people."

Now that we know this, step back and review the situation. The umbrella arrived in England. Objectively speaking, it was a perfect solution to a common problem. It's simple to use, easy to store, protects against the weather, and could be made widely available in an exceptionally rainy place. But our human brains are not governed by logic. They are governed by loss aversion, which is therefore how the Brits evaluated this new object. They had a positive association with rain; they believed it made them sturdy and robust. The umbrella, then, would interrupt that relationship with the rain, and therefore diminish their study robustness. They saw loss, not gain.

Of course, fighting the umbrella turned out to be harder than fighting actual rain: At least the clouds eventually empty. The umbrella stuck around for decades until another important change happened. By the early 1800s, London developed a street culture. Shopping districts became fully formed, and people moved among the shops and conversed outside. When it rained, nobody wanted the party to end. The umbrella, therefore, was ready for its moment. It was no longer an object of loss. Now it was the driver of gain.

This leads to a challenge for us all: When change impacts us, how can we see past the loss—and anticipate the gain?

In Search of the Good Stuff

When Kahneman and Tversky debuted their theory in 1979, it altered the field of behavioral science. Loss aversion became a fundamental concept, and as I noted earlier, decades of science has since been built upon it. Some studies challenged or confirmed the original theory; for example, in 2020, the study was replicated by studying more than 4,000 people in 13 languages across 19 countries. (The results were the same as they were in 1971.) Others have tried to understand how loss aversion impacts our decisions, and then how to steer us toward more logical choices.

This is a fascinating, messy, sometimes self-contradictory body of work—because people, of course, can be described the same way. But here are three findings from the past decade that I think can help us understand how to shift loss to gain.

1. **We need some good with our bad.** Researchers from the Wharton School and Harvard Business School were trying to solve the greatest riddle of politics: Why is it so hard to pass good laws? "Policies that would create net benefits for society that contain salient costs frequently lack enough support for enactment because losses loom larger than gains," the study says. Unfortunately, we can't just elect braver leaders. So how do we get better laws? The study found that when related bills are bundled together—one that involves a loss, like a ban on logging that would lead to job losses, and one that involves a gain, like an increase in public park land—they become more palatable and are easier to pass. (This was published in the journal *Organizational Behavior and Human Decision Processes*.)

2. **We're motivated by less loss.** When you're negotiating a contract or deal with someone, and neither side wants to budge, then you have reached what prominent Israeli lawyer Yair Livneh calls the "loss aversion obstacle." Both sides see their concessions as losses, and they do not want to lose any more. But multiple studies have identified a way out of this—and it begins by remembering that people feel loss more than they feel gain, and therefore both parties are focused more on protecting what they have rather than gaining new things. "[Make] a concession in a part of the deal where the other side stands to lose ground, rather than making a concession on a term that already stands to improve the other party's

position compared to the status quo," Livneh writes. "The most effective concession—the one that will add the most value to the other party for a given size of concession—is that which cancels a specific loss." (This was published in Harvard Law School's *Harvard Negotiation Law Review.*)

3. **We're irrationally attached.** Have you ever tried to sell an old object on eBay, but nobody wants to buy it? This could be why: You like the object so much that you think it's worth more than it is, according to Brigham Young University marketing professor Tamara Masters. Economists call this the "WTA-WTP disparity"—in other words, the difference between what you're Willing To Accept and what someone else is Willing To Pay. To confirm this in a study, Masters and her colleagues gathered up more than four hundred participants, and ran them through an exercise designed to make them feel attached to a mug. Then they asked these people to name a selling price for the mug. People who said they felt attached to the mug asked an average of $6. People who were unattached asked for an average of $4.77. When someone became attached to the mug, their cost of losing it went up. (This was published in the *Journal of Neuroscience, Psychology, and Economics.*)

What can we learn from all this? In short, humans are a bunch of nonsense—but at least we're predictable. The less we focus on loss, the clearer we can make decisions. If we are to become more adaptable to change, then the question becomes: How can we get ourselves out of this trap?

We must extrapolate the gain.

Our natural tendency isn't just to identify loss—it's to extrapolate that loss. We lose X, and therefore we will lose Y. Earlier, for example,

John Philip Sousa did it with recorded music: Some musicians' jobs will be lost, therefore he believed that *all* musicians' jobs will be lost, and therefore there will be no performances in the home, and therefore children will grow up to be machine babies. Then, as I described in the beginning of this chapter, it happened with novels: Children enjoy novels, therefore they are not spending every hour with their friends, therefore they will become delinquents. We do this on an individual level, too: If one thing changes at our job, we feel like everything will change, and then we fear we'll become useless and unable to keep up.

This may be our natural way of thinking, but it is not the *only* way of thinking. We can push ourselves to extrapolate gain, too. When we are faced with something new, we should ask ourselves these guiding questions.

1. What are we doing differently because of this new thing?
2. What new skill or habit are we learning as a result?
3. How could that be put to good use?

A brief personal example: I spent my twenties longing to live in New York City, then got a job there at twenty-eight and declared that I'd never be happy anywhere else. I married. I had two kids. We squeezed into a small Brooklyn apartment. Still, I said: I would never be happy anywhere else. At age thirty-nine, a pandemic arrived, and my wife and I decided to take shelter with my parents in Boulder, Colorado, where there was a lot more room for our boys to run around. I spent the first few months dismissive of the place; all I could see was the loss of my old life. I spent my days working nonstop. Then, one day around noon, I saw a neighbor ride by on a bicycle. He has a busy job; I asked how he has time to take a bike ride. His answer: "I can work another time." Then he rode away.

I kept up my normal routine, but now my body felt different. I could feel myself slumping into my chair. A question gnawed at me: *Could I also work another time?* In my entire career, I'd never taken a midday break. But one day shortly after that conversation with my neighbor, I did it. I got on a bike in the middle of the day and rode for an hour. It felt liberating. It was the stress reducer I didn't realize I needed. A new habit formed. And I felt the extrapolation of gain, through those questions I asked above:

1. *What am I doing differently?* I am rearranging my day.
2. *What new skill am I learning?* How to build self-care into my life.
3. *How can that be put to good use?* I am learning to do better work, with less chance of burnout.

This is how change can be additive in our lives, and why we must be so open to its potential—in even the most intimate ways. But I want to acknowledge something: This is not an easy process. It is rarely as straightforward as simply asking yourself three questions (even if they're useful questions), and then coming away with a new life philosophy. Loss can be real and difficult to manage. Some changes will come easier than others. Riding a bike in the middle of the afternoon is quite different from uprooting your life or switching careers, and change also does not happen in a vacuum: The shifts in our lives are subject to other shifts. Changes will compound. And sometimes, the best we can do is to act like Indiana Jones when he walks the invisible bridge.

Do you remember the scene? It comes near the end of *Indiana Jones and the Last Crusade,* when Jones is racing to save his dying father. He is on one side of a chasm; on the other side is the magical grail. There seems to be no way across, but then Jones remembers learning that, at some point in this quest, he will need to take a leap. It is a "leap of faith," he says to himself. He steps out into the chasm, with nothing but certain death beneath his feet—and lands firmly on an invisible bridge. There's good reason that this became an iconic scene: It is a metaphor for something we all feel at some point, as we walk into the unknown with little more than the belief that there is ground beneath our feet, and a hope in the reward across the bridge.

I'm not suggesting that you throw your full body onto that invisible bridge. But I do think you can put a toe on it, prove to yourself that something is there, and then find your footing. That is the gain.

Elana Pruitt is a good example of how this messiness can unfold in very personal ways. Years ago, she was feeling unhealthy and worn down. Someone suggested that she try changing her diet; maybe going vegan would help? That sounded like a big commitment, but she and her boyfriend decided to give it a try anyway. They made black beans, rice, and plantains for dinner one night, and thought of it as a little experiment. They felt good and decided to keep going. But soon, a thought started to terrify Pruitt: If she keeps this up and actually changes her lifestyle, she will lose large parts of her life.

"At the time, I just wanted to bar hop on Sunset Boulevard, live freely, and crash on the couch eating ice cream and cookies with my boyfriend before walking to the corner market in Koreatown for more booze," she told me. "We loved LA nightlife, so the idea of making conscious choices about food in particular seemed like a drag at the time, too much work, and a total killjoy."

Veganism also seemed to have professional consequences. She was working as a fashion writer, but felt like, if she went vegan, writing about leather boots and jackets would be hypocritical. "I started to feel lost about the direction of my career," she said.

There's that feeling—loss. This change in lifestyle might have been good for her, but it was hard to see the gain when she extrapolated everything she had to lose. Changing what she ate became equated with abandoning everything fun about eating. Changing what she wore equated with abandoning all her career goals. "I can see now that my thoughts came from a place of fear and long-standing insecurity," she said. "I suppose I just wanted to fit in everywhere I went."

Sometimes, we are not ready for one change until we experience another. It's like buying a new couch for your home; the addition doesn't make sense until you move things around to accommodate it. And for Pruitt, motherhood was that additional change. She had a baby boy, Qeshaun, about a year and a half after starting her veganism experiment, and that reoriented everything. She no longer needed to cling to her LA nightlife, which was now going the way of diapers and lullabies. She no longer needed to identify as a fashion writer, now that she experienced the larger identity shift of motherhood. She and her boyfriend stopped thinking of veganism as an experiment and considered it a permanent change. "My purpose became clear to me," she said. Pruitt started writing about veganism instead of fashion, branded herself online as Cool Vegan Mama, and is now building a business around the content she produces and the brands she represents. And just as importantly, Pruitt can still go out and have fun.

If you were to tally up all of Pruitt's gains and losses, you could technically fill both sides of the list. She lost an old identity, a familiar social life, and foods and habits she enjoyed—and at the start, she extrapolated that loss and feared having no identity, no social life, and no enjoyment. That's not what happened, though. Instead, all those categories were either adjusted or upgraded: She gained a new identity that was built off the best of her old identity, a different social life that better suited her new phase of life, and she found new foods and habits to enjoy. The losses didn't feel like losses because they *weren't*. They were gains in the making, but they couldn't be seen immediately. That is why, when we extrapolate loss, we must counter it by extrapolating gain.

The Good from the Seemingly Bad

Now let's zoom back out from the personal, so we can see how we all experience change together. Consider the novel one more time. People of the nineteenth century worried about its addictive, transportive qualities. But the result was extraordinary. I spoke with Leslie Butler, an associate professor of history at Dartmouth College, who specializes in American thought and culture in the nineteenth century, and she said the novel is now viewed by historians as "an important tool of sympathy or empathy." As the novels became more popular, antislavery and human rights movements also developed in America. Scholars debate exactly how much these two are related but agree that, as Butler says, "reading a novel enters you as a reader into the interior subjective life of other people—sometimes people like you, sometimes people not like you. It allows people to have this kind of psychic and empathetic identification with other people."

Critics of the time focused on the novel as a new habit-forming tool. What they missed, when seen through the lens of the three questions I asked above, was that it (1) presented readers with unique insights into others, which (2) helped them develop empathy, which (3) helped them support important movements toward equality.

Today, video games have replaced the novel as one of our objects of concern. What might we gain from them? First-person shooter games have been accused of making children violent—and although there's no reliable research proving that, there *is* research showing that the games help children think about objects in three dimensions just as well as academic courses on the same subject do. (Want a well-paying career in engineering, architecture, or other fields? This is a good skill to have!) In another study, role-playing games were found to help children develop problem-solving skills. "Video game play may provide learning, health, social benefits," reports the American Psychological Association.

And what happens when we extrapolate this gain? We see that gaming benefits may go even further—transforming not just how individual people learn, but also how groups of people work together. Hamza Mudassir, a researcher of disruption at the University of Cambridge, and founder of a company called Platypodes that helps companies manage moments of disruption, started exploring that possibility during the brief rise and fall of GameStop in 2021. If you follow the stock market, you surely remember it: Reddit and Discord users organized to inflate the value of GameStop—and then some other stocks, including BlackBerry—which sent traditional investors scrambling. Commentators wondered if the event was simply one-off chaos or a power shift in the markets. But Mudassir had a more intriguing take. He thought video games played a role in all this. Here's a bit from a piece he wrote, which I published on Entrepreneur.com:

> Both Reddit and Discord have their roots in videogames, where rapid discovery of information and coordination between multiple parties is essential to win. Most [self-directed investors] are millennials and Gen Z's, two generations raised with multiplayer games as their primary source of entertainment. Other than training millions on how to maximize the utility of tech platforms such as Robinhood, videogames also taught them how to build strong communities digitally. Games, like World of Warcraft, are known for their long-running clans and guilds—with millions being loyal to each other without ever meeting one another.
>
> Hence, from an anthropologist's point of view, it is not surprising at all that the combination of technology and digital camaraderie has allowed these disparate [investors] to trust each other and coordinate investment activities that have shaken the incumbents to their core.

Here you can see Mudassir extrapolating the gain: (1) Video games created a new way for users to interact, which (2) taught them to coordinate en masse despite loose ties, which (3) enabled them to disrupt the normal operations of the stock market. Sure, market disruptions aren't exactly a universal gain. (I speak from experience, having lost about $1,000 on BlackBerry stock by joining the shenanigans.) But it isn't hard to imagine how this new, collective skill set could be put to good use, too—driving new forms of communication, innovation, emergency response systems, and more. Those are things we'll never be able to appreciate, let alone foster and participate in, if we're too caught up in what we're losing.

We can even see this play out with video meetings, which were once considered a poor substitute for in-person meetings. When AT&T tried to sell the first video phones in the 1960s, it was an absolute failure. Even decades later, nobody understood the technology's purpose. "Seeing somebody almost destroys the intimacy of the communication," a former AT&T employee told the Associated Press in 1988, in a story about why the phones never caught on. By the early 2010s, even as we embraced FaceTime on our iPhones, we tended to think of video as a casual medium for purely casual purposes. Professionals continued to fly across the country just to sit in a room for thirty minutes with someone, thinking that was the only way to do meaningful business. Then during pandemic lockdowns, when we were unable to travel, we realized just how completely fine it was to not physically meet someone—and how, in fact, this option could even be better.

John Berkowitz, cofounder and CEO of the online real estate company OJO Labs, discovered this when he tried to acquire a Japanese brand in 2020. Japan's business culture is driven by relationships, and a deal of this kind would have previously required Berkowitz to repeatedly fly from his home in Texas to Japan for formal meetings and high-stakes dinners. But because of the pandemic, he had to meet everyone through

Zoom—and that, to his surprise, worked to his advantage. "It's hard to build a relationship in a boardroom," Berkowitz told me, "but when you are in your house, and your kid busts in and the internet goes out, we all get to know each other a little bit more intimately." Relationships were built. The deal was sealed. Nobody got on a plane—meaning that Berkowitz got to spend more time with his family, saved his company money, and maybe even achieved a better result than if he'd done things in the way that was once considered superior.

When we feel loss, let's push ourselves to seek even greater benefits. Are they there? Are they a possibility? Can we even imagine them? If the answer to any of those questions is even a vague and speculative yes, then it's worth exploring the opportunities ahead. We will always feel frozen by what we might lose; that is our nature. But belief in gain—even if we don't know exactly what it looks like—is the only thing that can truly propel us forward.

chapter 4

Use Yesterday for What It Was, Not for What It Wasn't

MICK used to bill himself as "your favorite brand's favorite DJ," and he earned the slogan. When Twitter or Adidas hosts a party, they hire him to man the turntables. LeBron James, Michelle Obama, and Prince have also been clients. MICK is an intimidatingly cool guy—hipster beard, designer clothing, an encyclopedic knowledge of music—and when we were introduced by a mutual friend a few years ago, I honestly wasn't sure we'd have much to discuss. I just am not that cool.

But we found much in common talking about dreading change and his looming crisis. His career is going great, but really, he wondered, how long can he keep at this? The life of a DJ happens on the road and at night, but he has a young son at home that he doesn't want to be absent from, and he's in his early forties, when late-night parties start to wear a little thin. MICK has big ideas, he told me—to expand into other entrepreneurial ventures, so that he's not just the guy who plays music. But he was nervous pursuing any of this. "I know this sounds stupid," he said, "but I feel like my success was based in part on luck. What if I can't repeat it?"

With thoughts like that, even your favorite celebrity's favorite DJ starts to sound like everyone else at the party.

Dig into anybody's future plans and you'll hit some version of this anxiety. It's always there, aching and sometimes paralyzing. It is our worry that we are not equipped to handle change—that, yes, maybe we did it once before, but what if our past success was just the product of luck, or chance, or good timing? What if we cannot repeat it?

I've felt this many times myself. I remember being at my first magazine job in Boston and being offered the chance to move to New York and work at the much bigger magazine *Men's Health,* and almost turning it down. I'd made good friends and done good work in Boston. *What if I'd lucked out?* I wondered. *What if my success was specific to this moment, and not able to be repeated?* But I was young and always wanted to live in New York, so I decided to take the chance. It was the right call: I went to *Men's Health* and also made good friends and did good work. And then, wouldn't you know it, the cycle repeated a few years later: I got a job offer from the business magazine *Fast Company,* and hesitated. *What if the past two jobs were luck?* I wondered. *How many times can I really roll the dice?*

I'll tell you something I've learned from experience: Those worries are toxic garbage.

Culturally, we talk a lot about taking responsibility for failure. It's a good message: *No excuses! We need to own our mistakes!* But we forget to own our successes, too. Our confidence should build upon itself—knowing that we only start from scratch once, that we have what it takes, and that our past simply shows a way forward. To do that, we have to start looking at ourselves differently.

For example, let's take a closer look at MICK.

MICK is his all-caps stage name, but his real name is Mick Batyske. He did not originally aspire to this life. "I had no intention of pursuing music as a career," he says. He DJ'd as a way to earn money and put himself through grad school in Cleveland, where he got an MBA in marketing—and because he was good at pumping life into a party, he soon became the go-to guy for the local clubs and the Rock & Roll Hall of Fame. When the Cleveland Cavaliers drafted LeBron James in 2003, the team was readying for a spotlight it had never experienced before— and Batyske figured their game-time entertainment could use an upgrade. He combined his music skills and marketing background, and pitched the team on an entertainment makeover. It worked. He became the team's official DJ, where he got to know the players, as well as the managers for sponsors like Nike and Pepsi. That's what shaped the career he has now.

When Batyske looks back at his younger self, he sees a kid who was in the right place at the right time. That's partially true. But there's no one definition of "the right place at the right time." You might be in the right place, at the right time, right now—but if you aren't able to recognize and capitalize on it, then it just looks like "nowhere special at no particular time." When I hear Batyske's story, I hear about a guy who understood how to identify and maximize opportunity, as well as how to combine innate creativity with marketing savvy. That's not luck; those are skills! They're also transferable skills. If Batyske hadn't landed the Cavs, he would have landed something else. And in fact, a few years after we spoke, he proved it: In addition to DJ'ing, he's now also a startup investor and advisor, and, along with his wife, Carolyn O'Hare, the co-founder of a brand consultancy called the Xavier Company.

Moments of change can trigger self-doubt. It's hard to look at our own story and separate our skills from our luck. But we can. And it starts by remembering the things we've forgotten.

A Longing for What Never Was

We have a strange relationship with our past.

Let's start with a simple example: Imagine that a kid returns from summer camp, and you ask them how it went. They'll give you a list of things that happened—half good, half bad. Six months later, ask them again about summer camp. Now their list of good things has grown, and their list of bad things has shrunk. Ask again in another six months, and they'll only remember the good.

"They don't remember their summer holiday—they remember their *idealized* version of a summer holiday," says Johan Norberg, a Swedish author and historian of ideas, including most recently the book *Open: The Story of Human Progress,* who described this scenario to me. "And that's the same thing with us as individuals as well."

You might reasonably call this *nostalgia:* The child has a sentimental longing for something from their past. Everyone experiences this in some form, whether it's nostalgia for our childhood, past jobs, past relationships, or something else.

Why do we do this? That's a complicated question, and scientists have tried to answer it for centuries. In the seventeenth century, when the word *nostalgia* was coined by a Swiss physician, it was often understood to be a kind of mental disorder. But today, science sees it quite differently: "Nostalgia has a lot to do with making us feel better *now,*" says Felipe De Brigard, a Duke University associate professor who studies memory and nostalgia. For example, he says, think about what you do with old friends. Some of your time is spent reminiscing about good times from the past, or even laughing about the bad times. Similarly, we celebrate anniversaries. If we are happily married, we may often reflect on our wedding or other happy moments. This is purposeful. "It's an act that has emotional repercussions *at the time* of engaging in that act," De Brigard said. By thinking fondly of the past, we feel more connected and grateful in the present, strengthen our bonds with others, and gain purpose for the future.

Our brains are programmed to do this—we retain the good emotions from good memories much longer than we retain the bad emotions from bad memories. (It's called *fading affect bias*, and I'll get into it more in Chapter 16.) This comes with some funny side effects. "Oftentimes we feel nostalgic for events that we did not like at the time," De Brigard said. "I think about my high school—I hated high school. I was bullied. I was not popular. And yet, sometimes I find myself daydreaming with nostalgia about high school. Like, *why on Earth?*" The answer may be because his hatred for high school, true as it was at the time, is not helpful to him *now*.

But while there's no harm in remembering high school more fondly than we experienced it, this kind of thinking can work against us in more profound ways—because when we long for the past, we may start preferring it over our present or future. At the most extreme level, demagogues from Hitler to Pol Pot have appealed to nostalgia by promising a return to some romanticized past. But even on a more casual level, entire cultures can be infected with the story of "the good ol' days"—a time before theirs that was better, and more wholesome, and more prosperous, and that should be preferred over whatever modernity promises.

This informs the way individual people think. Some of our assumptions about the world are based off whatever our community believes is true—and if we're surrounded by the belief that yesterday was better, we'll become less open-minded to future opportunities. Also, when we forget the challenges of yesterday, and simply believe that yesterday contained more opportunities than today or tomorrow, we become more likely to believe that our success was the product of circumstance. That may be the foundation of Batyske's fear (and my fear, and your fear). It can be paralyzing.

Before we go further into understanding ourselves, we need to escape this bigger myth. Let's look squarely at the supposed good ol' days—that mysteriously alluring time, either for an individual or an entire society, when everything was just *better*. When exactly was this time, and what created it? That's a good question. And it's a question I'm now going to take absurdly seriously, in the service of disproving it.

If the good ol' days existed, we should be able to look back in history and identify them—not just in the faulty memories of people today, but in documented evidence produced by the people who lived *during* those good ol' days. It should be waiting for us in the record books—an acknowledged golden age where happiness prevailed. So starting with the present day, I worked backward with the help of some very smart historians. I wanted to identify if, at any time in the last five thousand years, people recognized that they were living in a golden age.

The most recent major example of someone pointing to the "good ol' days" was Donald Trump's campaign slogan, "Make America Great Again," which was generally seen as referring to the 1950s. I asked Doug McAdam, a professor of sociology and political science at Stanford University who studies the era, if that was a golden age. And he firmly said, no. Some of the reasons are obvious: fear of nuclear war, extreme racism and sexism, and so on. But we forget that America was also terrified of itself, with new technologies like TV altering culture. "People talked about how mindless the students on college campus were—only tracking towards a conformist, consumer-oriented way of life, without soul," McAdam said. The people of the 1950s believed the pre-crash 1920s were a golden age—so I dug into periodicals of the time, and found people telling a very different story. This was the dawn of electricity, and people feared a life that was spinning out of control. "It is the day of the fleeting vision," *The New York Times* reported in 1923, for example, in a story that was common for the time. "Concentration, thoroughness, the quiet reflection that ripens the judgment are more difficult than ever."

What then? Rewind to the late 1800s, before electricity and cars and all those fast-moving things. Did those people believe *they* lived in a golden age? No: They believed they suffered from a disease caused by the modern world—literally nostalgia in the form of a medical diagnosis. "Nearly any type of condition that made life somewhat unpleasant could be attributed to neurasthenia," said David G. Schuster, an associate professor of history at Purdue University Fort Wayne and author of a book called *Neurasthenic Nation.* This led them to all sorts of wild medical treatments (and the birth of the concept of a wellness retreat), and they often demonized modernity. These people believed that America's pre–Civil War era was a golden age . . . but did the people of *that* time agree? No. They all worried that "the republic that the framers had created in the 1770s had decayed," says Harry L. Watson, a professor of history at the University of North Carolina at Chapel Hill. Leaders like President Andrew Jackson "wanted to get back to the good old days," Watson says, and Jackson often claimed that his ideas would be endorsed by the founding fathers—which was ironic because one of the fathers, James Madison, was still alive, and repeatedly said that Jackson did *not* represent the founders' original views. But no matter: The majority of the nation believed Jackson.

So if antebellum America looked back to revolutionary America, then when did the American revolutionaries believe a golden age occurred? Thomas Jefferson and his ilk idolized the Anglo-Saxon constitution of the medieval era. Was that a golden age? Not with the Vikings around! "You're living in this world in which these brutal pagan invaders are constantly destroying your crops, killing your family, and wrecking the religious institutions that define your life," says Andrew Rabin, the scholar of medieval law and literature who I quoted earlier in the book. As a result, the Anglo-Saxons' poetry is often centered on nostalgia for an earlier, unspecified time. A few hundred years later, the Renaissance might have seemed like a golden age . . . but "the Renaissance was just constant death," said Sarah Ross, a professor of history at Boston College.

War, plague, you name it. Renaissance intellectuals adored the ancient Romans; they often looked to Rome for models that might be useful in resolving their own terrible predicaments. But the Roman historian Tacitus can tell you how Romans felt about Romans: They thought their culture was overly violent and overindulgent. Alex Dressler, an associate professor of classics at the University of Wisconsin–Madison, told me that every Roman generation just idealized a previous, supposedly purer Roman generation. So if that was no golden age, let's rewind as far as we can—to the cuneiform texts of Mesopotamia, roughly five thousand years ago, where, yes: "We have quite a few texts where we find this idea of a golden age expressed in very clear terms," says Eckart Frahm, a professor of Near Eastern languages and civilizations at Yale University. In one story from the time, a creature with a fish's body and a human's head and feet pops out of the water, teaches people everything they needed to know, and then disappears. The moral of the story, as it was written, was that humanity has learned nothing since.

Conclusion: The "good ol' days" were never better than our own. They contained good times and bad times, solutions and problems, victories and setbacks. The human condition, on both large and small scale, is one of complexity. It's true for large-scale events, and it's true for individuals as well. Our past was not, and is not, the only good time.

As I researched this history, however, I spoke with someone who offered an important word of caution. He is Alan Levinovitz, an associate professor of religion at James Madison University, and he's done a lot of writing and thinking about the damage that nostalgia does. "I used to think that the way to undermine narratives that distort is to just rub people's faces in it," he told me. "Just force them to confront their own irrationality." Then he came to realize that nostalgia is often born of great pain; it's the product of someone coping with change and loss. "When you walk up to someone who is in great pain," he says, "and you rip away from them *the* key story that is keeping them from just dissolving into a puddle of suffering, you're messing with people when you do that."

What should we do instead? How can we help people who are trapped by nostalgia, if not to destroy the story? His answer: "You gently and tactfully allow them to take away their own narrative at a pace that won't cause pain. We either have to be patient, and work slowly at the parts of the narratives that are most pernicious, and work gently and tactfully and lovingly with the people who believe them, or we have to be damn sure that when we rip that narrative away, we have something awesome to fill its place."

These are wise words. To prepare for an uncertain future, we need to release ourselves from the rosy memory of our past—and begin to build a new, more durable narrative about ourselves instead.

How? Let's begin with the story of someone you may know, who just faced a transformation, feared it, ultimately embraced it—and in the process, rewrote her understanding of herself.

Kernel of Truth

Stacy London began her career in magazines. Then she was cast on a TV show called *What Not to Wear*, which ran for ten years, and she also became a visible spokesperson for Pantene, and this all transformed her into the kind of celebrity who people approached on the street to touch her hair. This shaped London's self-identity. She came to define herself as a television personality. But as she got older, the TV opportunities dwindled. A couple of years ago, she turned fifty and started experiencing severe perimenopause. She became acutely aware of the experience of middle age, and how it's rarely portrayed on TV or spoken about publicly. So she did what she'd done many times before—she pitched a TV show about it, in which she'd help women through the transition. It did not go well. "Everybody told me that it was unsexy and that nobody would watch," she told me. "Not only did I leave feeling like, 'Wow, they think I'm past my prime,' but I really went down this road of an insane and really crazy sense of worthlessness."

Meanwhile, a new brand called State of Menopause started creating products to help women manage menopausal symptoms. The company approached London about being a beta tester, and she threw herself into the work. A few months later, State of Menopause's parent company decided to offload the brand—and asked London if she wanted to buy it and become CEO, which she had no idea how to do. "I couldn't say yes right away," she said. "I really had to look at my own prejudices, which is that I thought 'I'm not good enough. I'm not smart enough. I'm not this. I'm not that.' But also, was I ready to let go of this idea of being a personality or a public figure? That's the vanity that I came up against."

This is the moment we've been discussing—when everyone, including people like Batyske and London, wonder whether their future can possibly be as bright as their past. "There was really, truly this moment where I thought, 'I don't want to be that person who is holding on to an old version of themselves,'" she said. "Because I have told countless people in their lifetimes, 'Let go of who you were to become who you are.' If I don't follow my own advice, then what the hell was I giving it to other people for?"

How did London make the transition?

"I kept asking myself, 'What is my kernel of truth?'" she said.

In other words, what old thing could she bring to this new identity? What did she *already have*? Being CEO would be new. Owning a business would be new. Being behind the scenes would be new. So what *wouldn't* be new? What did she already have that could help her cross this chasm? She called this her kernel of truth.

"I realized that my kernel of truth is my existential crisis," she said.

Her *personal experience* gave her an understanding of her customer. Similarly, she said, "I have always been a truth talker." People know her from TV as someone who's helpful but direct; she never hesitates to speak her mind. And isn't that what this new role required, too? "Why not take this on and speak truth about what menopause feels like and what it means," she said, "not just to middle-aged women, but to any person experiencing menopausal symptoms?"

London realized that, while there was much for her to learn, she already had some skills and assets that prepared her for this totally new life. She said yes to it. In early 2021, she officially announced herself as the company's owner and CEO.

Now let's unpack what London did, because it goes beyond identifying her kernel of truth. Unconsciously, London actually asked herself *three* important questions— and these are the questions we need to ask, too, if we're to liberate ourselves from nostalgia and build a new narrative of our lives.

Question 1: What did I overcome?

When you preference your good memories over your bad ones, you rob yourself of an important insight: You make your path look easier than it was. Now it's time to throw mud on your memories. What are you forgetting? What did you block out? What were the hardships and embarrassments that you overcame, which led to the success you've had now?

For example, when I look back at my first magazine job—the one in Boston that I was afraid to leave—I think about the great friends I made and the fun times I had. But as I sit here now, challenging myself to remember the hurdles, I'm finding things I was happy to forget. I often worked until 2 a.m., because I was such a slow and nervous writer. I once completely failed at editing a story, and another editor had to take over. A staff writer yelled at me after I changed something in his story, and we didn't talk for weeks. The fashion editor's very first words to me, the first time I met her, were "Why aren't you wearing a belt?" I strove. I stumbled. I often felt like an outsider. I embarrassed myself many times.

Why is it important to remember these things? Because it means the experience wasn't just a product of "good timing." It was a challenge. Success was not assured. Which leads to . . .

Question 2: What skill set did I have then that I still have now?
When you remember your earlier challenges, you can start remembering how you overcame them. How did you get through that mess? How did you win people over? Why did you succeed where others did not? The answer to this isn't luck. It is *you.* You have an innate skill set, but you may not even fully appreciate what it is. Now let's find it.

First, put aside whatever you think a "skill" is, because you don't want to define this too narrowly. I remember meeting a guy who spent his career writing movie reviews for newspapers, and then nearly every newspaper laid off their staff movie reviewer, and now he has absolutely no idea what to do with himself. What's his problem? He thinks that his skill is "writing movie reviews." Wrong. This is the problem of defining your skill by the action you take. Instead, I challenge you to think a level deeper: What is the skill set that *enabled* you to do your job?

For example, let's dissect me: How did I succeed at that first magazine job, despite having no real idea how to be a magazine editor? You might say it's because I was an innately good writer and editor—but I don't really think so. I was young and inexperienced. I wrote a lot of garbage. And when I struggled to write or edit something, I was too embarrassed to ask for advice. I also never read books about how to write or edit, or attended any conferences on the subject, because I just didn't think they'd be helpful. What did I do instead? I remember this very clearly: I obsessively studied great versions of the things I wanted to create. I bought stacks of magazines, laid them out on my bed, and inspected them. I broke each story apart—why did that sentence make me laugh, and how did the writer pivot from one subject to another, and why is this story structured this way? I wrote down the patterns I noticed. Then I applied what I'd observed to my own work, saw what worked and what didn't, and adjusted. That's because my skill set, I've come to realize, is not writing or editing. My skill set is *pattern matching*. I can look at a wide variety of something, identify the traits they have in common, and then repeat those traits myself.

We all have something like this—the skill that enables more skills. Batyske's DJing skills are incidental; what he's really good at is identifying opportunities and applying a sharp marketing eye. London's TV work was just one application of her skill; what she really does is channel personal experiences into relatable communications. You have something like this, too. I am sure of it. Maybe you are a fast learner, or an empathetic relationship-builder, or a keen organizer of information.

Now, think about the challenges you identified in Question 1. You overcame them because of the skill set you identified in Question 2. This is a version of your "kernel of truth," as London would say. You still have that skill set, and it will be with you no matter what transformation you go through.

And that's not the only thing in your arsenal. It's time to ask . . .

Question 3: What do I know now that I did not know then?
You are more powerful, knowledgeable, and wise than you were before—and you may not even realize it. Imagine marrying that wisdom with the innate skill set we just identified above! It's a potent combination.

Now let's identify what your *new* strengths are. What are you *even better* equipped to do today than yesterday?

This is another reason we identified your past challenges in Question 1. In the process of overcoming them, you transformed into what you are now. So rewind your memories, and ask: What did you lack before? What did you learn along the way to success? What are you more confident in doing now that you weren't so confident in then?

London is a great example. She was thirty-three when she got the job on *What Not to Wear,* and she'd never done television before. How'd she get the job? She had great knowledge of fashion, and she was personable and good on camera—all useful skills! But once she was on set, she realized she lacked something: She wasn't *comfortable,* and she had no idea what people actually wanted from her. "I really felt like I was supposed to act like I knew everything—that I was the authority, and I wasn't allowed to make a mistake and I couldn't make fun of myself because the audience expected me to be an expert," she said. "And halfway through, I started to realize: Nobody gives a shit. What they want to know is, *will this help them or not?* Nobody cares whether I'm an expert in this field or not. I was so on my high horse about my styling capabilities, when that's not what makes people relatable. What really makes people relatable is being bad and good at things. Having flaws and having incredible traits about yourself."

London started letting her guard down. She became comfortable with vulnerability, recognizing that her openness would win her more fans. *This* is the thing that truly paved her pathway of success. It's what led to more TV shows, and a rabid fan base, and ultimately, the willingness to embrace a new career where she's talking about her own changing body all day. Fashion knowledge and camera-ready talent wouldn't have gotten her there alone. She needed to evolve.

We all must identify our version of this. We know something now that we did not know then. We just aren't good at seeing it, because our improvement was so gradual that we don't notice how we evolved. We can't recognize our new powers or our true potential.

That's why this three-question exercise is valuable. We are a potent combination of old and new. Our raw abilities had put us in a position to develop new superpowers, and now we're able to unleash them. That's how, like a real-life video game character, we continue to move through levels, upping the level of difficulty, until we're slaying dragons without remembering how unprepared we once were for the challenge.

Is there a little luck in every success? Sure. We all took risks in our careers, and, through some unmeasurable balance of skill and timing and good fortune, they paid off in ways that led us to where we are. But was it all luck? If we had to do it over again, is there a chance we'd end up as failures? No way. Luck just influenced the path. It shifted the winds. If luck had broken for me differently, I might not be writing this book for you now—but I am absolutely certain that I'd have found some other satisfying path and built some different version of success. I think the same is true for us all.

Once we appreciate how far we've already come, we can start to quell the Panic and move on to our next phase of change: Adaptation. We work with what we've got. Sometimes it's a lucky break. Sometimes it's not. The important thing is that we keep moving forward—and know that because we took one big step forward, and we did not fall down, then we will stay standing when we take that next step, too.

PART 2

Adaptation

In this section, we're going to examine our own relationship with change. The most important thing to learn: You have more control than you think.

To appreciate that, let's consider a downside of change that people talk about all the time: our supposed "addiction" to new technology. We speak of it with resignation, as if we are powerless to overcome it. But in fact, we have the problem all wrong. We have more control than we think.

"Addiction" is a common drumbeat taken up by some of the loudest voices in our culture today. During a conversation about technology on his mega-popular podcast, Joe Rogan said, "We've got a real addiction problem in this country." In a congressional hearing in 2021, U.S. representative Kathy Castor of Florida said that apps are "designed to be addictive." During his 2020 presidential campaign run, Andrew Yang said, "Our kids unfortunately are getting addicted to smartphones."

Examples like this are endless. The words *technology* and *addiction* have become linked, such that you probably haven't stopped to consider whether it's true. Don't we all check our email too much, after all? Isn't that addiction?

But if you call people who study addiction—which I did!—you'll hear something different. "A lot of the time, these concerns about things like internet use or social media use haven't come from the psychiatric community, as much as they've come from people who are concerned about technology use," said Liam Satchell, a senior lecturer in psychology at the University of Winchester in the United Kingdom, who specializes in methodology and mental health.

Satchell, like many of his peers, is alarmed at how the word *addiction* is used by people who have no background in mental health. There is no scientific consensus on whether technology "addiction" exists, or if it does, how to identify and evaluate it. Studies have come out claiming that broad swaths of people are addicted to technology, like one recently that said as many as 34% of college students are addicted to social media, but Satchell investigated the methodology of these studies and found them to be borderline nonsense. Researchers are just taking a standard set of questions used to evaluate substance abuse—like, for example, "How many times a day do you drink alcohol?"—and then swapping out some language, so that the question might become, "How many times a day do you check social media?" This overlooks too many other factors, Satchell says. For example, the hallmark of any mental health condition, including addiction, is that it negatively impacts your social, occupational, or family life—but how do we account for the fact that much of our social, occupational, or family life takes place on the internet?

Do people overuse technology? Of course. But that's entirely different from addiction, and this isn't just a matter of semantics. Satchell and his peers say that by misusing the word addiction—by pathologizing a common behavior—we risk significantly impacting the way people are treated. For example, I spoke with Joël Billieux, a professor of clinical psychology at the Université de Lausanne in Switzerland, who also works in the hospital system there. He often works with patients whose gaming usage appeared to be an addiction—but instead of focusing on the gaming itself, he's focused on what's underneath it. Some patients are often suffering from trauma or depression. When that's addressed, the gaming subsides. In such cases, the gaming was the patient's way of coping with a larger problem. But if someone were to believe that overuse of gaming was an addiction, and therefore the problem in and of itself, then they'd miss these other issues and possibly compromise the treatment of these patients.

Here's the reason I share this with you, as we begin the Adaptation section of this book. The story of tech addiction is not simply one about fears of technology, or a confusion between overuse and something more pathological. The story of tech addiction is a story we tell all too often, whenever change comes to us. And it goes like this:

Something is happening to me.

We tell large and small versions of this story. We tell personal and societal versions of this story. My job has changed. My neighborhood has changed. My relationship has changed. In each case, *something else* that is *outside our control* has gained *total agency* over the decisions we make and the world we live in.

This is a terrible story. It's a harmful story! That's because when you hear or tell this story repeatedly—*something is happening to me*—you create what psychologists call "learned helplessness." I first heard that phrase from Nir Eyal, a bestselling writer who specializes in what he calls "behavioral design," and whose books *Hooked* and *Indistractable* examine how to capture other people's attention and how to protect your own. Eyal hates the narrative about tech addiction because he believes it trains people to give up. If tech is "addictive," after all, how can we have any power? We are addicted! We must need someone else to help us!

"But when you call it what it really is—a distraction or overuse—then, *Oh no, well now I can do something about it,*" Eyal told me. "*But that's no fun. Now I actually have to change my behavior as opposed to just shaking my fist and hoping the politicians and the companies will do something about it."*

Eyal gave me an example: Why would a child spend all day playing video games? Is it because they're addicted?

That answer is too simple.

In the mid-1980s, psychologists Edward Deci and Richard Ryan developed what they call the "self-determination theory" of motivation. It identifies three innate human needs— competency, autonomy, and relatedness. We need these things to feel happy and in control, and students rarely have access to them. A classroom can make kids feel incompetent; the endless rules of school and childhood sap them of auton- omy; and the constant overscheduling of kids' lives can inhibit their ability to relate with peers on their own terms. So what do they do? They find autonomy, competency, and relatedness in a video game instead, where they can master the virtual world, do it on their own terms, and connect with their friends.

Therefore, if a parent wants to solve the complex problem of video game overuse, they cannot focus solely on the gam- ing itself. They must create an environment where their kid has more control over their lives.

As adults, of course, we *do* have more control over our lives. Things do not only *happen* to us. And as Eyal told me the example of kids and video games, I flashed back to a time when I seemingly struggled with an addiction of my own: I was hooked on Twitter. I checked Twitter every few minutes at work, and then carried that habit home with me, which aggravated my wife. But now that I'm thinking about those three psycho- logical needs—autonomy, competency, and relatedness— I'm realizing how little of them I had back then. The company I worked for at the time had strange and burdensome policies, like making everyone switch desks every few months, which stripped me of my sense of autonomy. My bosses could never agree on what they wanted, which meant they were impossible to please, which killed my sense of competency. And because I was so sour, I felt disconnected from most of my coworkers— which meant no relatedness. What did I do as a result? I found all those things on Twitter, where I felt in control, confident, and connected to a community.

Then . . . change came to me. I was fired. My boss decided (reasonably!) that I wasn't performing well and wasn't fitting in with the office culture. I was embarrassed about this at first, but then realized how freeing it was. I started doing work I loved, on my own terms, and I connected with others who had a similar passion. In turn, my Twitter use dwindled to near-nothingness. I put that energy toward more constructive pursuits, like learning all the things you're reading in this book. And the crazy part is, I could have started all that progress much earlier. I could have quit that job. I could have walked out anytime! But I did not, because I felt helpless, and feeling helpless leads to no action.

Things do not just *happen* to us. There is always something that we can control. We will experience change, but we can also be the instigator of change. We can be the thing that *happens.*

Now let's adapt.

chapter 5

What You Do, and Why You Do It

Why is change so difficult for us?

A biological hypothesis goes like this: We evolved to fear change, because change could mean death. For our ancestors, life spans were short, food was scarce, warfare was regular, disease was everywhere, and a large animal was always eager to eat you. Routine became a matter of survival. You learned what was safe and you stuck to it. Then we built the modern world and risk became something that's rewarded—but our bodies, trained by millions of years of evolution, still react to change as if it's life-threatening. A looming career shift feels the same as a tiger leaping from the bushes. As a result, we seek safety and comfort—even if those things hold us back from our greater goals.

How true is any of that? I'm not sure it can be proven definitively . . . at least, not in our own time. Our early ancestors *Homo habilis* appeared more than 2 million years ago, and scientists say that "behavioral modernity"—abstract thinking, the creation of art, the hunting of big game, and the other basics of human behavior—began about 50,000 years ago. That means our "modern" world is only a blip, and hardly enough time for our bodies to update their hardwired instincts. Maybe we can all check back in 2 million years to see how we're feeling.

But until then, here is a simpler theory about why change is so difficult. It's a three-step line of thinking that ends in an existential crisis:

1. Change is scary because it seems all-encompassing and permanent.
2. When change happens to us, we worry that *we* will be changed in an all-encompassing and permanent way.
3. If we change in an all-encompassing and permanent way, then . . . *who are we anymore?*

I totally get this. I've often felt this way, too, which is why I kept asking successful entrepreneurs about how they navigated (and why they often *pursued*) change. Virgin Group founder Richard Branson epitomizes this; his career has been defined by exploration, as he forged into dozens of industries as varied as music stores, health care, hotels, mobile phones, and even space travel. "People get so wrapped up in the day-to-day of what they're doing," he told me. "It's important to sit back and think about *why am I on this Earth?*" Experts I've spoken with added nuance to Branson's answer—showing that while a person's sense of purpose can help them navigate change, the change itself can also help people define their purpose. That's what best-selling author Bruce Feiler learned while researching his book *Life Is in the Transitions,* for which he interviewed hundreds of people who went through massive life changes (which he calls "lifequakes"), and then identified patterns in their experiences. "Ninety percent of the people that I spoke to said that they got through their transition," he told me. "And part of going through the transition is to find meaning in it. A lifequake is a meaning vacuum. And a life transition is a meaning-restoring mechanism. It is the way that we make meaning from the difficult or the wonderful or the complicated thing."

From all this, I came to a conclusion: We are not *what* we do. We are *why* we do it. Even as our jobs or lives change, and we may feel dislodged from the things we knew best, we still have innate skills, abilities, passions, and beliefs that define us. Which is to say: Change is *not* actually all-encompassing and permanent—but we must be able to tell which parts of us will change, and which parts never will.

The Difference Between *What* and *Why*

Most of my life has been about not being comfortable with change. I preferred to find an identity and stick with it.

In my early teens, that identity was as a Miami Heat fan. (I grew up in South Florida.) I wore all Heat clothing. I watched every game. And I despised all trades, because I liked my team just the way it was. One time my favorite player, Glen Rice, was traded for the powerhouse Alonzo Mourning—and even though it was an objectively great trade, I'd go to games wearing my Rice jersey and booing Mourning from the stands. Later I became a punk rock kid who despised when my favorite bands "sold out" (aka when they signed a major record deal, hopefully enabling them to make a living off the thing they loved to do).

When I look back on this now, I see an insecure kid who outsourced his sense of self. If I didn't know who I was, I could at least subsume myself inside something more established.

By early adulthood, I thought I'd gotten over that. But I didn't. I graduated from college and got a job at a small newspaper—and then that became my identity. I subscribed to three daily papers. I spoke incessantly about newspapers, and read books about newspapers, and many of my friends were newspaper reporters. Then, after a few years, reality set in: Newspapers were a struggling industry where layoffs were constant and the hours were terrible. This caused me some panic: *If I'm not a newspaper reporter, then what am I?* My identity felt shaken.

I eventually figured out the answer: I should be a magazine editor. Then I repeated the process. I got a job at *Boston* magazine, subscribed to a dozen magazines, spoke incessantly about magazines, all my friends became magazine editors, and so on. There was nothing else I wanted to be. Nothing else I needed to be. *I was a magazine editor.* Until . . . reality eventually set in there, too. I took a few more magazine jobs, and discovered that I didn't always love the work. Sometimes I considered leaving. And while I ultimately stayed, my job evolved to where I'm no longer simply a magazine editor. This again caused me some panic: *If I'm not a magazine editor, then what am I?*

Then I started spending all my work time talking with entrepreneurs. That's when I learned about a new way to think about our identities. Entrepreneurs don't define themselves by *what* they do. Instead, they identify an abstract mission and then figure out endless ways of accomplishing it.

This is the difference between your *what* and your *why.* It's also the difference between feeling lost amid change, and feeling like you can survive anything.

Here's an example. Foodstirs is a sweet baked goods company that originally just sold baking mixes—you know, bags of powder that transform into delicious brownies and cakes. The business launched in 2015 and grew fast, thanks to a powerful cofounder trio: experienced food industry exec Greg Fleishman, actress Sarah Michelle Gellar, and PR industry veteran Galit Hadari Laibow. Around 2019, the trio began prepping for a transformational moment: They were going to start selling packaged goods like brownie bites and mini doughnuts, which had the potential to redefine the company. A lot of money and effort and time went into this, and Foodstirs planned to roll out their new products nationwide in the beginning of 2020 . . .

Then, of course, the pandemic hit. Baked goods sales plummeted nationwide, and baking mix sales soared. (After all, parents needed something to do with their kids.) Foodstirs had a hard decision to make: Do they still go ahead with their transformative product launch, just as they'd planned, or do they shelve the whole thing and double down on their old version of themselves? They chose the latter. More than a year's worth of planning evaporated. During all this, I talked with Fleishman. "Were you bummed to have to abandon these plans you worked so hard on?" I asked him. He paused to think. Then he said, no. "It goes back to why you start a business to begin with," he told me. "Our mission is about upgrading sweet baked goods and bringing joy to people's lives. We're doing that now."

Foodstirs doesn't just make baking mixes. It creates joy with sweet baked goods. To Fleishman, that's the only thing that matters—and there are endless ways to do it.

This was a new way of thinking for me. But the more I talked with entrepreneurs, the more I heard about it. LinkedIn cofounder Reid Hoffman, for example, advises that people live in a state of "permanent beta." Usually, we talk about *products* in "beta"; it's the phase when something is being tested and refined. What if *people* lived like that? What if we considered ourselves to be forever a work in progress? If that were the case, change would never feel like failure. Instead, failure would feel like data.

Eventually, I came to understand exactly how entrepreneurs developed this flexible way of thinking. They began by identifying something at their very core—a purpose or mission that is so foundational to their businesses and their lives that absolutely nothing could change it. This was *why* they did something. Then, depending upon the opportunities and resources available, they'd find different ways of articulating their why. This became their *what*.

Consider it:

Foodstirs sells baking mixes. That is *what* the company does. It is changeable—in demand one day, perhaps not in demand the next.

Foodstirs brings joy to people's lives. That is *why* the company does it. It is not changeable—if one method of bringing joy stops working, there's always another.

If Foodstirs' founders identified their mission only by their *what*, they would be lost. They'd think, *We make baking mixes*—and then, if people ever stop buying baking mixes, the company loses its purpose. But Foodstirs knows: The *what* is mere habit. It's an idea that makes sense until it doesn't. The *what* can fly away in the wind. But the *why?* The *why* is drilled into the ground.

We all have a *what* and a *why*, and we need them both, but we cannot confuse them. We are not knocked down by something as flimsy as a *what*. We are the creators of infinite possibility. And it all starts by knowing what changes, and what never will.

Once I understood what entrepreneurs were doing, I wanted to identify my own *why*. So I created the following exercise that helped me dig into myself, layer by layer, and liberate myself from my own identity crisis. It can help you do the same thing. We're going to run the same scenario three times in a row—and each time, we're going to go a layer deeper until we discover a clear summary of your true mission.

Layer 1: The surface

Imagine that someone comes up to you at a dinner party and says, "So what do you do?" Write down your answer in a single sentence.

Likely, you're going to talk about your tasks. This is how we tend to explain ourselves—we say *what* we do at work. For example, you might say something like, "I'm a project manager at a toy company, so my job is to work with lots of different teams and get the product out on time and on budget."

For me, I once would have said: "I'm a newspaper reporter, so I go out and interview people and then write stories about what's happening in my readers' community."

Now let's go deeper.

Layer 2: The mantle

A person comes up to you at a dinner party and says, "So what do you do?" Now you're not allowed to repeat anything that you said in the first round. Instead of talking about your tasks, think about the skills required to do them. These are the things that people don't see, and maybe don't even understand, but they rest underneath everything you listed out before.

If you're a project manager, you might say: "I use my organizational skills to keep track of everything that's going on, my communication skills to deal with the needs of many different teams, my management skills so I can handle the many different needs and motivations of the different teams I'm working with, and my learning skills so that I can become fluent in what all my teams are doing even if, frankly, I don't know how to do their jobs."

For me, when I was a newspaper reporter, I would have said: "I follow my curiosity to discover new things, then engage people in conversation to learn information, and then I'm able to think and write quickly in order to process that information into a comprehensible narrative for readers."

Why did we just detail our skills? For two reasons: First, because it genuinely is helpful for us to pause and identify what we're good at. And second, because we are programmed to identify ourselves by our *what*, we need to slowly and methodically step away from it, so that we can get to our core—to our *why*.

Layer 3: The core

One more time: A person comes up to you at a dinner party and says, "So what do you do?" Now you're not allowed to repeat anything that you said in the first two rounds. No tasks. No skills. Instead, ask yourself: *What fuels me?*

This isn't an abstract question. This is the singular idea or belief or goal that excites you—and that led you to develop the skills you just described, which enabled you to do the tasks you originally identified with. This is the thing that could excite you even if you didn't have the job you have, or the job you wished you had. It could fuel twenty different jobs, maybe even in twenty different industries.

What is it? Try to write it in ten words or less. Start with the word *I,* and then only describe things you have full control over. For example, the statement "I sell houses in Coral Springs, Florida," is full of too many *whats.* Your real estate agency could close; you could move out of town. You need a phrase that can withstand outside forces.

This is going to be a very personal answer. Maybe a project manager would say, "I love helping people achieve things." Or, "I'm a logical thinker and I love solving complex puzzles." Or, "I'm a builder and I want to build great things."

It took me a while, but I eventually figured out this answer for myself. Here's my sentence:

I tell stories in my own voice.

That's my *why* in seven words. And each word matters. Notice how I said that I *tell stories,* rather than that I *write.* That's a major departure from when I defined myself as a newspaper reporter, and then a magazine editor. I realized that I'm just as satisfied writing for magazines as I am making podcasts, or talking on a stage, or creating a video, or developing a TV show, or writing this book. The phrase *in my own voice* is also critical to me. There were times during my career where I lost all passion for what I was doing, and that was scary. If I didn't enjoy being a magazine editor anymore, then I had no idea what I was. As a result, I stayed in some jobs I didn't enjoy, or took assignments that made me unhappy. But now I understand the problem: I hated executing someone else's vision and writing in somebody else's voice.

No longer. I'm done with that. I'm only happy if I'm executing *my* vision. If I'm lending it *my* voice. Sometimes, like now, that means you're reading the words I wrote, but other times, I'm happy shaping something with my sensibility and tone. I tell stories in my own voice. This is my core.

Understanding this was liberating.

Once I had this, I wondered how other people identify themselves. So I started asking some of the most successful people I met. Dwayne "the Rock" Johnson told me that, earlier in his career, he felt too restricted as just a wrestler or actor. He realized that he wanted to be "a ten-lane highway approaching the world," building a relationship with his audience that's unrestricted by product or medium. "When you find your voice and you know who you are, that allows you to soar," he said. His business partner and global strategic advisor Dany Garcia, who has developed or cofounded many brands with him, describes her own mission as "advancing the human experience"—and this big, broad thinking allows them to experiment and push into realms as diverse as ice cream, tequila, and the XFL. "We are not attached to process," she told me. "We are only attached to outcome."

You don't have to identify your *why* right away. You can work on it. Refine it. Adjust it as you go. When I spoke with Chip Gaines, who rose to fame with his wife, Joanna, on the HGTV show *Fixer Upper* (and they now run their own cable network, Magnolia, as well as a constellation of brands in different industries), he spoke of how difficult his identity crisis has been. "My life's most complicated struggle has been summarized by the thought that if you don't sweat, if you don't physically feel exhausted, you haven't actually worked," he said. Gaines began as a tradesman, building houses. Now he's building brands, which is a different kind of hard work—but it doesn't make his back ache. In his early TV days, this disconnect kept him up at night. He'd go out at 9 p.m. to do random chores with farm animals, just to feel like he'd *done* something. He still grapples with this today, but he said he's made peace with at least one idea: At his core, he can still be a builder . . . but now he is a builder of people and personal networks. The work he does creates livelihoods for others, and he and Joanna still do it all in their hometown of Waco, Texas, where their support systems are. "Building a network always felt like valuable work," he says. That's the mission at his core.

And here's one more: When Jimmy Fallon left *Saturday Night Live* in 2004, he tried to be a movie star. "If somebody had asked why that was your goal, would you have had an answer?" I asked him years later. He paused to ponder it. "No," he finally said. "I'm trying to think, why would that be my goal? Maybe, from all the books and articles that I'd read, the trajectory of someone famous from *Saturday Night Live* is to do movies. It's just the path." Want to hear the opposite of a self-directed mission? Four words, right there: "It's just the path." Not *your* path. Simply *the* path, *a* path, *some* path. Perhaps as a result, Fallon's movie career flopped. He moped around for a while. Years later, he took over the 12:35 a.m. show *Late Night*—and a few years in, he figured out his why. It is this question: "Can it make people happy?" That simple insight helped him understand his purpose, and it now guides everything he does, from hosting *The Tonight Show* to producing new shows, writing kids books, making new products, and more.

Once you find your *why*, you will always have an anchor like this. You will know what fuels you no matter what.

This is what it means to adapt to change. It means knowing what changes . . . and what does not.

chapter 6

Widen Your Bands

Most people make bad predictions and then move on, never to speak of them again. Very few write mea culpas later. But that's what newspaper columnist Mickey Guisewite did in 1999, after initially dismissing a newfangled contraption called the internet. "When I first started hearing about the Internet a few years ago," she wrote in a column at the time, "I could spend hours and hours pooh-poohing it to a wide network of family, friends and coworkers."

She was, she explained, once "one of millions of passionate nonusers of the Internet." Then her friends became internet-savvy and she became lonely and unplugged. "Something's gone terribly wrong here," she wrote, which is the closest thing I've ever seen to a technophobe's cry for help. "The Internet was supposed to become obsolete—not people like me."

Today, of course, Guisewite is more than obsolete: She's a prehistoric bug frozen in amber. But let's be generous to her. Guisewite, like everyone, lived through many supposedly "transformational" moments that turned out to be duds. Perhaps she was worried in 1976, when televangelist Pat Robertson said that the world would end in 1982. (It didn't!) She might have spent a lot of money on eight-track tapes (only to see them replaced by the cassette), or laser discs (replaced by DVDs), or Blu-ray discs (which never toppled DVDs). Maybe she took jobs that didn't work out, or dated people who were duds, or moved to cities that failed to live up to her expectations.

Like us all, in other words, Guisewite learned that not *every* opportunity will work out, and we cannot waste our lives chasing them all down. We must filter. Perhaps Guisewite did that in earnest. Then she filtered out the internet.

This book is all about finding opportunity in change—but Guisewite stands as an important cautionary tale. Change isn't all good. It isn't all useful. But some of it is life-altering in the best ways. So how can we figure out *which* change to embrace? Which job do we take, or which place do we move to, or which thing do we spend time learning?

When most of us try to evaluate the future, we rely on very unscientific observation strategies—like we "feel" that one decision is better than the other. This means we're just evaluating our own experience. And sadly for us, we are not always the best judges of our own options.

There *are,* however, professional judges of opinions, and I talked to one of the most accomplished. His name is Warren Hatch, and he's the CEO of a highly sought-after forecasting company called Good Judgment, which takes a methodological approach to predicting the future. If you were a plastics manufacturer who wanted to know about the global need for plastic in five or ten years, you might hire Good Judgment to tell you. The company is staffed by people it calls Superforecasters, who have special abilities to predict the future—but not in a storefront psychic kind of way. Rather, they're able to dig into data and see what nobody else sees.

When Hatch wants to hire Superforecasters for his company, he looks for people who are good at looking beyond themselves. They must be excellent at pattern-matching, open to ideas that feel conflicting, and be "cognitive reflective"—in other words, they challenge themselves on whether their answer is the *right* answer. But most important, he says, they cannot be overconfident.

"Most people are very overconfident," he said. "If they have a view of the world, they'll defend it to the death." But most people are unaware of their overconfidence. Without realizing it, they limit the number of factors they'll consider or they won't naturally engage with the possibility that they're wrong. And this is why he tests people for overconfidence.

When I heard that, I of course wondered: Am *I* overconfident? I don't think I am, but then again, maybe that's my overconfidence speaking. So I asked Hatch for an example of how to test for this.

Then he asked me one of the questions from his test: "What year was Gandhi born?"

Before I go on, I encourage you to pause and ponder this question yourself. Do you know when Gandhi was born? If not, great: Please guess along with me, as Hatch is about to ask me two follow-up questions. You may be just as surprised as I was—not necessarily at the answer, but at *how* you answer.

Here we go.

I told Hatch that I had no idea when Gandhi was born. He said that's fine. "What's the earliest you think he was born?" he asked.

"I guess . . . 1940?" I replied.

"Now what's the latest you think he was born?" he asked.

"Um, 1955?"

Then Hatch told me the answer: Gandhi was born in 1869.

I was ashamed of my answers when I said them, and I am ashamed now to be memorializing my ignorance in this book. But what came next was so valuable that I cannot let my shame get in the way—and it's the reason I wanted you to play along as well.

"That's OK!" Hatch told me. "It's not important that you know when Gandhi was born. What's important is to know how confident you should be in the knowledge you think you have."

Consider what I did, he said: Even though I was given the option to create any range of dates I wanted—picking the earliest and latest possible years that Gandhi was born—I picked a range that was only fifteen years wide. I decided that Gandhi was born between 1940 and 1955, based on nothing. "You have your bands too narrow," Hatch told me. "You should want to have wider bands."

Now I understood. I didn't want to admit my ignorance, so I made what amounts to an all-or-nothing bet. "What I should have done," I said to Hatch, "is I should have thought, 'I don't know anything about Gandhi, so the earliest he was born was 1600 and the latest he was born was 1980.'" Hatch smiled and nodded in agreement. Yes, had I done that, even though I would have displayed no useful knowledge about Gandhi, I would have answered the question correctly. I would have created a range that included his birth year.

Why did I not do that? I asked him.

"Because you're overconfident!" he said. "Now you've learned. And the next time you're confronted with something, you'll be cognitive reflective and you'll go, 'I don't know that much; let me widen my bands.'"

"This will sound like a stupid question," I said, "but what's the value of widening my bands?"

"Because if you are overconfident in what you think you know, you're going to be making decisions informed by probabilities that are not going to align with reality," he said. "And they compound. So if you make a decision—*well, I know this*—and then you make another decision based on that decision, you can find yourself really far out on a statistical limb, needlessly so. The value is to slow yourself down so you can get to a better outcome."

And how do we slow down and get to a better outcome? We get out of our own heads, and into someone else's.

Other People's Problems

Katy Milkman is like a walking, talking library of every smart study ever done about behavioral change. She's a professor at the Wharton School at the University of Pennsylvania, whose research focuses on how insights from economics and psychology can change people's behaviors in positive ways. (She also wrote a book called *How to Change*.) After talking to Hatch, I called her to ask the question I'd been puzzling over: In a world of infinite options for change, how does someone identify the *right* change for them?

"The first thought that comes to mind is a really famous case study of Andy Grove and Gordon Moore," she said.

Moore was a cofounder of Intel; Grove was its president in the 1970s and later became CEO. Today Intel is a technology giant, and the world's largest semiconductor chip manufacturer by revenue. But in its early days, Intel made its name by producing low-cost memory chips. Business was good until the mid-1980s, when Japanese companies began making cheaper and better chips—and Intel's fortunes fell. One day, Moore and Grove were sitting around at the office trying to figure out how to save their business, and Grove asked Moore a question: "What would happen if somebody took us over, got rid of us—what would the new guy do?"

"Get out of the memory business," Moore replied.

Grove agreed. So why wait for someone else to do it? The two men resolved to do what their successors would have otherwise done—and that meant making massive, painful changes. They laid off more than seven thousand people, shut down plants, and pivoted Intel into the microprocessor business. That decision saved Intel.

Milkman likes this story because, she says, it's a good example of taking an outside perspective to a very personal problem. "There's a fair amount of research suggesting that taking an outside perspective can make you more dispassionate, a clearer thinker, a better observer," she says. "When we're thinking about someone else's problems, they don't feel so personal. We don't escalate commitment to an already chosen course of action. We can see the pros and cons more clearly."

But of course, it's not easy to get outside your own head. So Milkman offers these three strategies.

Tactic 1: Copy and paste

When Milkman and her collaborator Angela Duckworth teach classes, students often ask them for guidance on how to do better. In turn, the professors ask this question: "Have you asked your friends who are doing well in the class what's working for them?"

"We get a lot of blank stares," Milkman said. "People rarely really deliberately tap into the sources of information in their social networks." This is a big mistake. "A vastly underused strategy, which is the simplest of all, is copy-and-pasting things that have worked for other people."

Milkman and Duckworth's research backs this up. For example, they gave different advice to two sets of students. One set was told to make a simple plan for increasing their exercise. The other set was told to identify someone who has good exercise habits, ask them what their strategy is, and then simply copy that strategy. The students who copied strategies had improved outcomes.

This sounds so obvious, so why don't we do more of it? Milkman says it's because of something called the "false consensus effect"—a scientific term for people's belief that everyone thinks the same way they do. As a result, we fail to realize how much new knowledge is stored in our friends', families', and acquaintances' heads.

"If you're thinking about how do I make a change, or what's the right change," Milkman says, "try to think, 'Is there social information I can gather from other people who've pursued a similar path or faced a similar dilemma or actually made these changes? And what can I copy and paste that worked for them?'"

Tactic 2: Give advice

If you're feeling lost, you may not feel best suited to give someone else advice. Wrong: You are *exactly* the right person to give advice.

Milkman points to research done by psychologist and assistant professor Lauren Eskreis-Winkler, who has investigated the nature of success by studying failure. She found that when people give advice to someone facing a similar situation, they become better able to tackle the problem themselves. Why? First, giving advice builds confidence: When someone comes to you for help, you feel like you're in a position of power and that your ideas are valuable. Then, it forces you to introspect more deeply—thinking about your own issues and what you need. Finally, there's the "saying is believing effect." You start to suggest things that you yourself might not have thought to do . . . and then you want to do them, too.

"Once we suggest them, we start to believe them," Milkman says. "We start to feel hypocritical if we don't do them. So it's this magic sauce where you get yourself to get behind a risk that you wouldn't necessarily be comfortable telling yourself to take. And then in the end, you convince yourself to take it."

Tactic 3: Pre-mort your decisions

Most people in business have participated in a "postmortem." It's that strange term borrowed from the world of autopsies, when people at a company discuss what went well and what failed in a project that just ended.

Milkman suggests doing a version of this *before* you make a change. This comes from work done by author and former professional poker player Annie Duke, who wrote a book called *How to Decide,* which highlights the power of negative thinking. People tend to lionize positive thinking, but Duke argues that negative thinking can give us more clarity around likely barriers and obstacles that we're going to face. The process helps us feel more prepared—but also helps us think more realistically about what risks and challenges we're willing to tolerate.

Hatch of Good Judgment also suggested pre-morting your decisions, and he added a useful layer to it. He suggests that people ask themselves, "If I made this decision, and six months from now I'm regretting it, why might it be? What is the thing I'll look back on and go, 'Gee, I wish I had not missed that'?"

Of course, you could go overboard with pre-morting. You could imagine the worst-case scenario for every option, and then talk yourself out of doing anything at all. That's not constructive. As you enter this process, both Milkman and Hatch said, you have to accept that no option is perfect. Every change is coupled with unpleasantness. The goal of a pre-mort isn't to avoid discomfort; it's to help us weigh our options and select the risks we prefer to manage. "That can be a great way to help give definition to your thought process, as well as uncover hidden assumptions that are going on, that you can bring to light and help you think through more carefully," Hatch says.

Through these three tactics—copy-and-pasting other people's strategies, giving advice, and pre-morting our choices—we're extracting ourselves from our own minds, and just as importantly, from our own limitations. We push ourselves to think more clearly, and to look at our own choices with fresh eyes.

Will the right change become immediately evident? No. The future is unknowable, even to a Superforecaster. But you can, as Hatch and Milkman agree, cut down on the noise—and eliminate the greatest obstacle to decision-making.

Choice Overload

Our lives are full of noise, but we often don't recognize it as noise. Instead, we think of it as *choice.*

To be clear, there is nothing wrong with having options. Choice is great! Who doesn't love lots of different foods on store shelves, and movies available to stream, and friends to see, and people to date, and paths for career advancement? These things make us feel good, because it means we can customize our lives and pick *exactly* what we want. And all this choice—this abundance, really—is the result of people responding well to changes in their lives and in society. We have new things because someone, somewhere, decided that the status quo wasn't good enough, and other people agreed, and innovation followed, and it resulted in choice.

But research shows that, in truth, we have a complicated relationship with choice. Columbia Business School professor Sheena S. Iyengar captures this nicely in a series of studies, which highlights what she calls "choice overload." In one famous study, her research assistants posed as employees of a fancy jelly company, and set up a sampling table at an upscale grocery store on two Saturdays. The number of choices offered would alternate every hour throughout each day. One hour, they offered customers 6 flavors of jelly to sample. The following hour, they offered 24 flavors. The 24 jellies attracted more people—60% of shoppers stopped to taste them, compared to only 40% who stopped for the smaller group. But when it came to actually *buying* the jelly, things were different. Of the people who sampled a jelly, only 3% of people bought anything from the group of 24 options. However, 30% of people bought from the group of 6 options.

What happened? People had so many choices that they simply could not choose. The choices became noise, and they had no way to filter it.

This is the problem that Hatch's company Good Judgment is constantly trying to solve. Hatch says that, above all else, a Superforecaster's greatest skill is the ability to filter out noise. "There's a lot of information out in the world. There's no shortage of opinions out in the world," Hatch says. "How do you filter those out and zero in on the diagnostically useful—both for the questions you need to ask, and the forecast that you will focus on?"

When we're trying to make personal decisions—weighing multiple options, evaluating which change to take—we often create a lot of this noise ourselves, Hatch says. That's because, at any one moment, we're often considering two different kinds of factors: There are the things that are genuinely important to us, and there are the things we happen to be thinking about in the moment. I remember experiencing this when my wife and I looked to buy our first apartment in Brooklyn. We had infinite options to look at, and as a result, we had trouble identifying exactly what was important to us. One day, I became hyperfocused on having more outdoor space. The next day, all I cared about was built-in air-conditioning.

To help separate what's important from what's not, Hatch suggests making a pro/con list. That may sound lame and obvious, and Hatch agrees: Making a pro/con list actually *isn't* all that useful . . . until you make many of them.

Hatch suggests making a pro/con list about any change you're considering. Then set it aside. Wait a week. Do not look at your old list—and then, make another one. Repeat a few more times if you'd like. "Now look at it and see how many of them overlap," he says. "Did some of the pros show up regularly? Or did some of them cross over to a con? If half of the things that were on the first list are gone on the second, then you might consider those things to be noise."

The more we can filter our own noise, the more we can focus on what truly matters to us. Then our decisions become clearer.

You can go a step further than just putting ideas down on a list—and instead, put some of them into action.

"This is going to sound like the weirdest piece of advice," Milkman tells me, "but one of the things we do too little of when we're trying to figure out the right change or the right next step is experiment." Pick one of the things you're weighing, and just try it. Sign up for a class in something you're interested in, or, if you're at a company and weighing a career change, ask your boss if you can take on some additional responsibilities. "Pull the trigger on *something* because we tend to experiment too little. We tend to explore too little."

Why don't we do more of this? Milkman says it's because we fear a premature permanence. We think of any change as a lasting one—which means that if we alter our job, for example, we're now stuck with it and have forever altered the course of our career. But that's not the case, Milkman says. "We need to be more comfortable actually labeling it: *This is an experiment*," she says. "It's not the end. It's not my end goal. I'm exploring."

Want to filter the noise? Add data. That's what an experiment is, after all.

When we face down multiple options for change, we may often feel like we're looking into parallel universes—worlds where we're suddenly transformed in different ways, and we cannot imagine or access those worlds without fully submitting to them. But that's not true. Everything in this chapter proves otherwise. We can test our ideas against the real world by giving advice to others, asking successful people for their strategies, or just tentatively trying something new and adding to our own personal experience. We can identify what matters to us by bouncing our thoughts off other people, and, with something as simple as multiple lists, bouncing those ideas off ourselves, too.

There is no way to make a perfectly informed, completely safe, 100% guaranteed correct decision. But there are ways to challenge ourselves, and be aware of our limitations, and expand our minds—and in the process, gain clarity on what's best for us. The process of choosing the right change, in other words, also requires us to change.

chapter 7

Change Before You Must

People love a cautionary tale, and there is no greater cautionary tale than Blockbuster.

But when we tell the story of Blockbuster, we often get it all wrong.

Here's the story as we think we know it: Once upon a time, relaxing evenings began at Blockbuster. You'd drive to the nearest location, wander its aisles, pluck a movie off the shelf, grab some microwavable popcorn, and check out using your membership card. Then you'd drive back home, insert your VHS (or eventually DVD) into a machine, and settle in.

Sound inconvenient? Not at the time. It was the height of convenience. Blockbuster even had a little slot at the front of their stores, so you didn't have to enter the building when you returned your movie the next day. (You didn't want to get hit with a late fee!) In 2004, Blockbuster Video seemed unstoppable. It had approximately 9,100 stores across the world. It *owned* home entertainment.

Then Netflix appeared. Blockbuster didn't see it coming. The end.

That's the story we tell: Blockbuster *didn't see it coming*. Couldn't have imagined the benefits of home delivery or streaming. Didn't think Netflix stood a chance. This is a story of arrogance and stagnation. It's a story of the dummy CEO who could not see the future.

But that's a counterproductive story to tell. When we say "that CEO is stupid!" we're really just giving ourselves comfort. We're saying: *Bad things happen to dumb people, but not to me!*

Wrong. It could happen to you, too. Because this story is a lot more complicated.

To start, know this: The people at Blockbuster weren't dumb. John Antioco was CEO from 1997 to 2007, which was the company's most eventful decade. He joined after saving two well-known brands. First, as CEO of Circle K, he took the company out of bankruptcy, built it back up, and sold it to the oil company Tosco. Then as CEO of Taco Bell, he turned a shrinking brand into a cultural giant. He joined Blockbuster because he saw a lot of opportunity there, and he executed on it. He changed its financial arrangement with movie studios (which massively boosted the bottom line), eliminated late fees (which made customers happy), and invested heavily in a Netflix-like online DVD subscription service (to prepare for the future). Under his leadership, Blockbuster nearly doubled revenues to $6 billion and reached its peak of power.

But he didn't have the right support. Viacom, which owned 80% of the company, wasn't interested in his pivot into the digital space. Blockbuster became public, with most of its stock held by hedge funds. Carl Icahn, the famous activist investor, bought millions of shares himself and effectively controlled the board. In a piece for *Harvard Business Review*, Antioco describes what it was like working with Icahn's team: "One of them had a bunch of ideas, such as putting greeting cards in the stores, carrying adult movies, and making a deal with Barnes & Noble to add a book section. Mostly, though, they questioned our strategy, which focused on growing an online business and finding new ways to satisfy customers, like getting rid of late fees." Eventually Antioco was pushed out, and the company then hiked its online prices, cut its marketing, and pushed hard on the in-store business. The result: collapse.

In his *Harvard Business Review* piece, Antioco washes his hands of all this. He says he tried to pivot to the future, but was stopped by an institution that couldn't see beyond the immediate moment. Too many of its decision-makers were focused on maximizing *today,* instead of building for *tomorrow.*

Maybe that's true, or maybe they're the words of a seasoned executive trying to wash egg off his face. But either way, this much is undeniable: Blockbuster saw change coming and *couldn't do anything about it.*

This is what messy reality looks like. I said earlier that Blockbuster isn't a story of arrogance and stagnation, and it's not a story of the dummy CEO who can't see into the future. But the truth is messy, too. Imagine what true action would have looked like. It would have meant that, back in 2004, at the peak of Blockbuster's power, before the hedge funds and Carl Icahn started sniffing around, Antioco could have said, "These stores are making money, and things are going great, and now it's time to *shut them all down.* We must focus on the future."

That would have seemed like the most insane, reckless, delusional idea in the world . . . except that, in the end, it would have saved Blockbuster.

If we are to properly adapt to change, we cannot think short-term. We must instead play a long game—and accept that, for a little while, it's going to hurt. But it'll hurt a lot less than *not* adapting, and then running out of options.

It sounds difficult, but it's not impossible.

Playing the Long Game

You may not get to choose how your life will change, but you can choose how you react to it: You can either wait for change to impact you, or you can change on your own terms.

Both sound hard, but one of them is deceptively easy. Consider the options:

Wait for change to come to you.

Cons: You will be scrambling. Your hair will feel on fire. Everything you built will be threatened, and you will need solutions fast.

Pros: You can claim that it's not your fault! Sure, your life will feel like it's in a tornado. The people who depend on you will be in a panic. You might suffer financially. Your relationships may be threatened. But you can say, "I wasn't trying to cause pain! This just happened to me!" And if you must make a difficult decision— disappointing friends and family, laying people off, eliminating something that other people love—you can at least say you did it under duress. But still . . .

Likely end result: You're done. Game over.

Now, consider the more proactive option:

You make the change first.

Cons: You will seem like a maniac because you will be *choosing* change . . . which often means choosing pain. You may be shuttering something that works; you may be laying people off, or leaving money on the table, or walking away from a seemingly golden opportunity. Things were going well for you, and now it will appear that you're hurting yourself even though nobody forced you to. You're doing it based on a belief, an instinct, a prediction.

You're not sure if you're right. Nobody's sure if you're right. And they are angry, because they cannot see what you see.

Pros: You may not know the right answer, but you do know this: If you don't do something *now*, then everything will fall apart. You're taking control, and you're doing it while there's still time. You are taking a bet—and bets are inherently risky!—but you do it knowing that a bet must be taken.

Likely outcome: You win the long game.

This is what it means to play the long game, especially when it hurts. It is possible. Here's someone who can prove it.

Planning for Failure

Sam Calagione is the founder of Dogfish Head Craft Brewery, a beer brand in Delaware. But for a while, he became known as the guy who wouldn't serve you your favorite beer.

To understand this story, you need to know two basic beer terms. The first is IPA: It stands for India Pale Ale, a very hoppy style of beer. The second is ABV: It stands for "alcohol by volume," or how strong a beer is. Budweiser has a 5% ABV. Coors Light is 4.2%. And back in 2001, Calagione made a beer that he called 90 Minute IPA, which is 9% ABV. This is a beer that puts you on the floor, but tastes surprisingly light.

People were digging the 90 Minute IPA, but Calagione's distributor gave him some feedback. They said, essentially, "This is great, Sam—but can you make a version that doesn't get you hammered?" So he did. In 2003, he created a tasty alternative called 60 Minute IPA, with a more reasonable 6% ABV.

People liked 60 Minute IPA. Then they loved it. Then they *demanded* it. Calagione's little brewery was getting calls from bars and restaurants and liquor stores nationwide. By 2006, 60 Minute IPA was a runaway hit, and on track to become 70% to 80% of all sales at Dogfish. That is to say: Even though Dogfish made many beers, the vast majority of everything it sold was going to be 60 Minute IPA.

Most entrepreneurs would be thrilled by this, and they'd sell it hard. After all, isn't this the point of business—to create things that people love, and then cash in? But Calagione thought differently. This hit product worried him, because he knew something: Change was coming.

Like everything else, beer trends come and go—blonde ales replace lagers, which replace stouts, which replace pilsners. The IPA was having a moment in the 2000s, but Calagione worried about what would happen if he let sales of 60 Minute IPA go unchecked. Every bar, and every restaurant, and every liquor store would carry 60 Minute IPA, and maybe only 60 Minute IPA, which meant that beer drinkers would start to think of his company as an IPA brand. That would be fine for a while . . . until tastes change. Then Dogfish Head wouldn't be thought of as an IPA brand. It would be thought of as an old brand.

That's why Calagione made a decision that sounds reckless and insane: He capped sales of his best-selling beer at 50% of all sales. Remember, this beer was on pace to become nearly 80% of all sales at Dogfish. Calagione just decided it would never go beyond 50%.

The result? People were furious.

I have walked the streets of Delaware with Calagione, and he is a legit celebrity there. People stop him to talk. At his brewery, they ask for selfies like he's Beyoncé. He has a Dogfish-themed inn just a few miles from the brewery, where beer lovers sit around the fire pit drinking his beers and telling tales about the time they met Calagione. But when Calagione made the decision to limit sales of his best-selling beer, that goodwill momentarily disappeared. People called Dogfish's headquarters and started screaming. Calagione remembers a local Delaware liquor store owner approaching him on the street, tears in her eyes, furious at him for withholding the product that her customers kept asking for.

I asked Calagione if this reaction ever scared him. Did he doubt himself? Did he worry he'd made the wrong choice? Calagione said no, never. He understood exactly what he was doing. He held firm. When Amtrak called and asked for 60 Minute IPA—a client most breweries would dream of!—he said no.

But he didn't *just* say no to these people. He offered free hats and an explanation. He said Dogfish makes its beer fresh, and he wants to provide only the highest-quality product. So while the brewery produced more of its hit beer, he suggested that people try some of his other styles of beer. Dogfish has many of them, after all, and all are great. Would this liquor store want to stock his Namaste White? Would this restaurant care for a keg of Punkin Ale? Amtrak ultimately picked up his 90 Minute IPA and became that beer's largest buyer. "We believe in this business model," he'd tell people. "Please bear with us."

This is how Calagione managed to introduce the full range of his beers to the world, instead of just his 60 Minute IPA. And in time, he was proven right: Tastes changed. Today, while IPAs remain popular, they don't attract the same fervor. And Calagione has benefited from the shift. Nobody thinks of Dogfish Head as an IPA brand. Instead, they think of it as an innovative brand. They flock to his Deleware brewery and inn—and now also the three restaurants he's opened in the state, as well as one in Miami—because they know Dogfish is always trying something new.

In 2019, Calagione got the ultimate financial validation: He sold Dogfish for approximately $300 million to the Boston Beer Company, the maker of Samuel Adams. The deal would have never happened if Calagione cashed out early all those years ago. An old IPA brand is not worth $300 million—not even close. But Calagione changed before he had to, which meant he did it on his own terms.

And he's not the only one.

Don't Wait for the Moment of Pain. Look for the Moment of Awareness.

Andy Monfried is one of those guys who speak in certainties. He has a deep voice and never minces words. When he says something, you think to yourself: *This guy is all in.*

"I don't want to be AT&T, still selling landline services in a world where wireless is coming," he once told me. "I don't want to be selling cable television, knowing that Netflix and YouTube and Roku and Amazon are coming."

It's easy to say those things. They sound obvious. But it's much harder to live those words. Plenty of people were selling landline services while wireless approached. Many are *still* trying to sell cable television, despite more than 20% of US households having cut the cord.

I'm one of those cord-cutters, by the way, but getting there was a classic moment of resisting change. My wife wanted to cut the cord for years, but I said no. I rarely watch TV, but I grew up with cable and something about it just felt comforting. I liked having *options.* What if a new show comes on? What if friends are over and want to see something? What if, what if? So I insisted we keep it . . . until one day, when we were flying on JetBlue and I had nothing to do, and I started flipping around on the in-flight TV. It had been years since I aimlessly flipped channels, and the experience was maddening. Every show was dumb. Every channel wasted my time. I felt enraged. The stupidity of it all! And then I realized: *Oh no. My cable subscription at home funds all this.* Then I turned to my wife and said, "We're getting rid of cable." We did it as soon as we landed.

I lost so much money on television I never watched. What I should have done instead is watch Monfried, because he acts today based on what's going to happen tomorrow. It's the reason that he killed off a healthy business that was making $30 million.

"People thought I was nuts," he says.

In 1997, Monfried joined a company called Advertising.com, which sold digital advertising. Almost every ad you see on a website is the product of some cockamamie system of middlemen. And back in the 1990s, Advertising.com was a middleman with its own cockamamie system. It would buy ad space from a publisher's website—so, for example, it might buy the rights to place ads in certain locations on nytimes.com, and it would pay for that space based on the number of impressions that ad would get. Then Advertising.com would sell that space to advertisers . . . but the advertisers would pay Advertising.com even more money, based on how many people *engaged* with the ad.

Buy low, sell high. This worked. But a few years into it, Monfried had a better idea. Back then, the internet was just developing into the data-sucking machine that it has become, and Monfried realized that this data could be valuable. He could identify internet users by demographic— say, just men between the ages of 25 and 35—and then show ads specifically to *them*. This is a common system today, but back then it was brand-new. Monfried knew that, if he could get it to work, advertisers would pay a premium to ensure that their ads were seen only by the people most likely to be their customers.

Monfried left Advertising.com and started a company called Lotame, which pioneered this idea of targeted ads. He sat down with brands' advertising planners and said, "Do you want to reach 35- to 45-year-old males who make over $100,000 and love baseball?" They'd nod. "Then," he says, "we would literally build the audience in front of them and show them those people and show them those targetable cookies and device IDs."

It was genius. Money started flowing. Within two years, Lotame had gone from zero revenue to $30 million, and Monfried had raised many millions of dollars from investors.

Then, one fateful day, he met with a brand's advertising planners.

These people had been spending hundreds of thousands of dollars a month with his company, but now they said, "I can't give you any more money. We're building what you're doing at our agency."

He left that meeting bummed, but not especially alarmed. OK, fine—one agency is copying his idea. But then he heard it from another agency, and he knew: His company was doomed.

Was Lotame still profitable? Yes. Would it likely be profitable for years to come? Yes. Not every agency was going to build its own data-tracking system—and even if it did, he was years ahead of them. People would still pay him. People would still want his service. But he knew: *They won't want it forever.*

If you want to find the moment when someone must make the most important decision of their life, it looks like this. It isn't at the moment of pain—it's at the moment of *awareness.* It's the first time someone realizes that their company is in trouble, or their career is in jeopardy, or their relationship is doomed, or their health is in decline. What happens next will define everything.

In this book, we've already covered what generally happens next: People panic. Then they either make a rash decision, or they do nothing.

Monfried didn't want to do either. But he knew time was ticking. He also knew that he didn't want to be selling landline phones in a cellular world, and he didn't want to be selling cable TV in a streaming world. Now was the time to translate those beliefs into action.

So he did. In the course of ten days, he came up with a new direction for his company, permanently closed his ad-targeting business, and laid off half his staff. This was emotional work. Laid-off employees were shocked and hurt; they'd done everything he asked of them. Investors were surprised; they'd invested in the plan he was now abandoning. People didn't understand what he was doing, or why he was doing it. He'd explain that the company was doomed, but people would say: *Where's the evidence? We're making money!* And that was true. "I really had no evidence to back up what I was saying, other than the fact that I was sitting in front of customers and hearing directly from them," he told me.

One of his investors suggested that he keep the original business open, to use it as a "cash cow" while he builds his next business. There's a logic to that. If the original Lotame was still profitable, why not keep that income flowing? But Monfried said no: That won't work, because companies naturally focus on wherever their revenue comes from. Everyone's attention would remain on the old idea, and they'd never build the new idea. It's impossible to starve a cash cow, Monfried said. Instead, a cash cow will eventually just starve *you*.

"In those ten days, I probably slept ten hours. And in those ten days, I probably lost twenty pounds," he said. He suffered with conviction. He helped every one of his laid-off employees find new jobs—it wasn't their fault, after all. Then he set about building a brand-new version of his company Lotame. In the old version of Lotame, he paid publishers for the rights to sell ad spaces on their websites. In the new version of Lotame, publishers paid *him* for help understanding their audiences. He took all his data-tracking know-how and repackaged it: Now he helps publishers gather and understand their *own* data, so that they can sell their ads themselves. It's a more stable business than his first idea, he says. When we spoke, he'd rebuilt that $30 million in revenue and then some, and was serving hundreds of clients, including giant names like Hearst, WebMD, IBM, and Bloomberg.

I asked Monfried what kind of leader he thinks he is, and he had a good term for it: "Ready, fire, aim." To him, time is not a luxury. It's fleeting. If he doesn't act immediately, he will fall behind.

Act on What You Know

It is not easy to change before you're forced to. You will never have all the evidence in front of you. You will never be able to plot the perfect course or identify your next move on a spreadsheet.

So how do you do it? I have a soft answer, and then a concrete answer.

The soft answer is this: You act on what you know. Calagione knew the beer world. Monfried knew the ad world. People may have been upset by their decisions, but those people did not know what Calagione and Monfried knew.

The concrete answer is this: You stress-test yourself. My friends Adam and Jordan Bornstein run a firm called Pen Name Consulting, and they do this with clients all the time. They identify weaknesses in businesses, and then play them out to the extreme. "If a door falls off your car, it will suck, but you can drive just fine," they once told me. "You can't say the same if your engine blows up. You need to know what are the doors, and what is the engine."

In other words, sit down and play everything out realistically. See what happens, and what's fixable, and what's not, and then act now to address future problems. Imagine, for example, that demand for *every* Dogfish beer started skyrocketing, instead of demand for one beer. At that point, if Calagione stress-tested his company, he'd see that he has a capacity problem—his facility wouldn't be able to create enough beer to meet future demand. In the Bornsteins' car metaphor, this problem is a door. It's fixable in a straightforward way; Calagione would have just needed to raise money and expand his manufacturing. But because Calagione's problem was a surge in demand for *one* beer, a stress test would reveal a risk to his reputation. That's not a door. That's an engine.

Another interesting self-stress test comes from the podcast company Wondery, which produced massive hits such as *Dirty John* and *Dr. Death*.

Jen Sargent started as the company's COO, and then, when Amazon bought Wondery in 2021, she stepped up to become CEO. When I spoke to Sargent a few months after the sale, I was curious about the tension inherent in her job—because Wondery, like any creatively driven company, must take risks that are hard to quantify, but it is now inside one of the most data-driven companies in the world. I imagined this is hard to reconcile. Data wonks might look at a popular show and then insist on making ten more shows just like it—and while that might produce some wins, it's also the kind of short-term thinking that leaves no room for experimentation, and therefore no ability to play a longer game. Creative work sometimes requires pushing out into the unknown, which cannot be market-tested the way a new Amazon Basics line of batteries can. So how does Sargent maintain a culture of innovation at Wondery, while also speaking in numbers?

"For brand-new things, especially content, it's hard to quantify the risk," she told me. So she pushes her team to take educated risks. "When there's a lack of data, one of my favorite sayings I've learned at Amazon is 'What do we need to believe to be true in order for this to work?' I love that because then it's like, *Oh, OK, I don't have all the answers, but here's what I think is going to be true.*"

"Can you give me an example?" I said.

"Yeah," she said. "We want to spend a million dollars on this new podcast idea to reach a new audience that we've never reached before. Is that worth it? Well, we don't have any data because we haven't launched anything in this space before. But we believe that, in success, we're going to reach two million people and it's going to generate X million advertising. And this is actually going to put us on the map to attract more talent that will attract more of these types of people, and let us launch more podcasts in this vertical. And in five years' time, we're going to have made $20 million off of this $1 million investment. And that's what I believe to be true."

Is it actually true? If she goes forward—which is to say, if she believes it to be true enough—then she will find out.

Although the door/engine and "what do I need to believe?" tests are both useful, they both also push us to think about things that are fundamental. We all know, almost instinctively, what we must do in order to play the long game, and we know when we have to do it.

The question we will ultimately be judged on is: Did we trust ourselves, and act upon that trust?

Keep that question in mind. In the coming chapters, as you learn to adapt and find a New Normal, that's a trust you'll need to build.

chapter 8

Work Your Next Job

My wife recently introduced the *Hamilton* soundtrack to our son, who now wants to listen to it on repeat every time we're in the car. That's fine. It sure beats the Pokémon theme song we once endured on loop. Like everyone else, I think *Hamilton* is a masterpiece—but there's this one moment that I always find grating.

The musical *Hamilton* is, of course, a Broadway retelling of America's founding fathers by Lin-Manuel Miranda, with a focus on the critical role played by the future first Treasury secretary, Alexander Hamilton. At the end of Act I, after the Revolutionary War is won, the founding fathers are debating the kind of government they'll build. Hamilton, James Madison, and John Jay decide to write essays defending the new Constitution and published anonymously, to push voters to ratify the document. In the musical, this becomes a brief but very dramatic moment. Aaron Burr says:

In the end, they wrote eighty-five essays, in the span of six months
John Jay got sick after writing five
James Madison wrote twenty-nine
Hamilton wrote the other fifty-one!

That last line is spoken with intensity, synchronized with soaring music, as if the very idea of it—writing fifty-one essays!—would be jaw-dropping to the audience. *That* is the part of the musical I hate. Why? Because if you're a writer, it is really not that hard to write fifty-one essays. (Even if, fine, they were historically influential essays.) I spend my days writing, and I'm currently editing a magazine and making podcasts and writing this book all at the same time, and I hardly consider it a feat of strength. But the musical treats this moment like Hamilton just killed fifty-one men with his bare hands.

One day, I told my wife about this objection. She wasn't having it.

"Hamilton was working his next job," she says. "Isn't that what you're obsessed with?"

This is true. "Work your next job" is one of my favorite phrases, and the guiding philosophy of my career, and a critical part of adapting to change. And as it turns out, my wife was right: That was exactly what Hamilton was doing. She promptly pointed me to *Alexander Hamilton* by Ron Chernow, the biography that the musical is based on, where the essay writing is explained in more detail:

For Hamilton, it was a period of madcap activity. He was stuck with his law practice and had to squeeze the essays into breaks in his schedule, as if they were a minor sideline. Robert Troup noted of Hamilton's haste in writing *The Federalist:* "All the numbers written by [Hamilton] were composed under the greatest possible pressure of business, for [he] always had a vast deal of law business to engage his attention."

In other words, Hamilton was a busy guy with a busy business. But he understood that the *most important thing* was also the thing he had the least amount of time for. So he made the time, and changed his life and America as a result.

The Paradox of Goals

In front of you right now, there are two sets of opportunities:

Opportunity Set A: This is all the work that's expected of you. It's your job responsibilities, and how your success is measured. The wonks would call this your KPI—Key Performance Indicators. Whatever you need to do to fulfill your boss's and anyone else's expectations, that is Opportunity Set A.

Opportunity Set B: This is all the stuff available to you, but that nobody's asking you to do. Perhaps these opportunities are at your job—they're new responsibilities you could volunteer for, or teams you could join, or skills you could learn. These opportunities may also be outside your job: They're a class you could take or a thing you try. Nobody in the world expects you to pursue these things; nobody is asking or even suggesting them. But they are *available*. That's Opportunity Set B.

Now here's what I'm saying: Every day, your time will be consumed by Opportunity Set A. You will be at work, and you'll be scrambling to fit everything in, but you will move with purpose because your incentives are all aligned around Opportunity Set A. This is where promotions come from, and where your boss's praise originates, and where you see upward mobility. But in truth, if you look at the long tail of your life, Opportunity Set A is actually the less important set. If you focus on Opportunity Set A, you will only be qualified to do the things that you're already doing.

If you want to succeed in the long term, and ride the waves of change, then Opportunity Set B is infinitely more important. It's where your true energy and passion should be. Your days should be devoted to checking the boxes of Opportunity Set A—after all, we have paychecks to earn—and then pouring your life into Opportunity Set B.

This is what I mean by "work your next job." While you are at your current job, you are laying the foundation for your next one. Opportunity Set B is where you learn new things and develop transformational new skills. And here's the most important part: When you pursue Opportunity Set B, you *do not need to know* how these new skills will pay off. You also do not need to know where your career is going. In fact, it might even be better that way.

I'll tell you a cautionary tale of someone who thought they knew exactly where they were going: It is the true story of "Tom," a real friend whose name I'm changing.

Tom always wanted to work at one specific company. He set this goal at the beginning of his career because that company was full of widely recognized talented people, and it produced products he thought were genius. Joining that tribe became his definition of success, and he would accept no other. Every job he took was strategically selected to one day appeal to his dream job. He followed the company religiously. He got to know people who worked there. He went out of his way to develop skill sets that were perfectly catered to what this company wanted. He did, in really every way, work his next job—with the singular focus on getting one job.

And after many years of labor, he got that job.

It was not what he expected.

It was gratifying in many ways, sure, but it was thankless in too many other ways. It paid poorly. The hours were awful. It was often creatively stifling. Tom stayed there for years, often deeply unhappy, because the idea of being there still gave him joy, even if the work did not. But eventually, he left. It was too much to take. He's held a series of impressive jobs since then—the guy is talented, after all—but he hasn't been passionate about them. He still does not really know what he wants, because he spent his entire career plotting one course.

I meet a lot of people who are like this. They made a critical error, which will sound counterintuitive: They stuck too close to their goals.

Why's that a problem? Malcolm Gladwell once gave me a great answer to that question.

Gladwell is the kind of guy that many journalists aspire to be—and I count myself among them. He became a name brand at *The New Yorker*, often considered the pinnacle of journalism, then wrote a series of best-selling books (*The Tipping Point*, *Blink*, and more), and now has a wide range of high-profile projects and surely makes gobs of money speaking.

I interviewed him years ago about his excellent podcast, *Revisionist History*, and I couldn't help but ask: How does he decide what a Malcolm Gladwell project is? This was a greedy question, because it was really for me. I wanted to understand how a guy like him makes work that is distinctive and coherent. He doesn't just do things; he does Malcolm Gladwell Things, and everyone recognizes them that way. What's the secret?

He replied that, to the best of his ability, he tries not to have an answer to this question at all. "The most important thing is never to make a decision about yourself that limits your options," he told me. "Self-conceptions are powerfully limiting. In the act of defining yourself, you start to close off opportunities for change, and that strikes me as being a very foolish thing to do if you're not eighty-five years old."

This was my friend Tom's error. He defined himself narrowly.

Should we have goals? Should we have some form of self-conception? Let's be real: We must. We'd be listless without them. Even Gladwell acknowledges that: "I'd like to pretend that the things I do can be different as anything under the sun," he told me. "Now, it's obviously not true.

But it's just really useful—more useful to think that way than to have a sense in my head of what I stand for." Indeed, we need something to move toward. We need an orientation point in the thick forest of our lives.

But while we move toward those goals, we should also prepare to abandon them. Something else better may come along—something that fills us with joy and curiosity, and that ultimately may be far more fulfilling than whatever goal we were working toward—and we must be willing to indulge that chance. We must accept that the greatest opportunities may be the ones we weren't looking for, and maybe didn't even know existed.

I meet so many entrepreneurs who laugh—laugh!—at the reality of what they're doing now. They say things like, "I never planned to run a soap company!" But that soap company pulls in millions and challenges them in all the right ways. They love that soap company. And they got there not through careful plotting, but by indulging the unknown. This is also, weirdly, the story of my marriage: My wife and I met on the dating site OkCupid (back when it was the cool option in pre-Tinder days), but she was filtering for men taller than me, because that's what she thought she wanted. I would have never shown up in her searches. Instead, I found and messaged her. We are the same height. She fortunately gave me a chance anyway.

Goals can be motivating but limiting. It is a direction but not a map, and it cannot define your whole journey. If you look ahead too narrowly, you'll miss all the promising off-ramps in your periphery.

This is why, when we work our next jobs, we should do so with equal parts focus and curiosity. We can't control our future. Remember the truisms of change: It's inevitable, it's unpredictable, but it's opportunity. When you expand your skill sets, you're simply increasing your *potential*—setting yourself up for multiple zigzag paths that can lead to an amazing payoff.

The Zigzag Payoff

What does a zigzag payoff look like? Let's say, for example, that you're an accountant who would like a new career, but you feel unqualified to do anything else. And let's say that you love comedy podcasts. What if you start your own comedy podcast? It will probably be bad—in fact, it will almost certainly be bad. Nobody will listen to it. So why do it, if you don't have a specific plan for how this comedy podcast will help you? Here's why: Imagine that, in the process of producing this very bad podcast (zig), you become very good at audio editing (zag)—and then, when a musician friend of yours asks if you can help them record something, you're able to do it (zig), and the recording sounds great, and then your friend tells their other musician friends about you, and soon you've got a library of new work, and then you're hired at a local studio (zag), and then you open your own studio (zig), and now you're a music producer with an entirely different career (and bonus, you can do your own accounting, so zig and zag!), and it's all because you created a crappy podcast that nobody listened to, and certainly that nobody asked you to make.

That is how to adapt to change—not by calibrating to it, but by becoming so changeable that your path evolves around any roadblock. If you're not exploring beyond your boundaries, you will become stuck inside them. Opportunity Set B is the greatest opportunity of your life.

I speak from experience. Here's how Opportunity Set B transformed me.

When I started my career in local newspapers, I looked around for models of success. What I saw were reporters who'd slowly climbed a ladder—starting at a tiny newspaper, then graduating to a slightly larger one, and onward until they'd stopped and settled down. One older colleague back then told me, "When you work in newspapers, you can afford the smallest house on a nice block." I don't mean to demean this—my colleagues were devoted to their communities and built happy lives. But I wanted a different path.

I wanted to make fast leaps. I wanted to go big. I also knew that newspapers were becoming unstable—change was coming!—and I didn't want to go down with the ship.

So I asked myself: *What do I need to get ahead?* Most industries, I'd been told, are about who you know. I didn't know any impressive journalists, and I was living in a tiny town in Massachusetts, so I thought email would be my only way to make connections. I started writing people for advice—reporters, editors, columnists, basically anyone whose work I liked. Many were generous with their responses, but they didn't take me seriously as someone to mentor or hire. In 2005, I managed to start a short email exchange with Allan M. Siegal, a legendary editor at *The New York Times.* When I told him that I planned to work at the paper someday, he replied, "With any luck, I'll be retired."

He meant it as a joke (I think?). But the implication was clear. I was a *very* long way away from being qualified to be his colleague.

After that, I gave up on emails. Instead, I broke my situation down into three categories that I've found helpful ever since: What I Have, What I Need, and What's Available. In my case back then . . .

What I Have: I have a job, but it's at the bottom of the ladder. This means I'm surrounded by people who are also at the bottom, and likely cannot help pull me up.

What I Need: I need to learn from better writers and editors. I need the experience of writing for bigger publications. I also need evidence of my skills—because sure, I believe in myself, but I have not been validated in the marketplace. Allan M. Siegal of the *Times,* for example, does not care about my stories in my little newspaper. People like him will only respond to stories in publications they consider to be their equals.

What's Available: Freelancing. Writers can pitch an individual story idea to an editor at a big publication, and if the editor likes it, they'll assign and run the story. These editors may not hire me right now, but maybe they'll take a chance on me writing one story.

That became the plan: I freelanced. I did it in the morning and the evening. I did it whenever I had a spare second at my office. Every day, my goal became to get my day-job work done as fast as possible, so that I could devote more time and energy to freelancing. I did this for years. And it worked. These clips helped me get job interviews, and then a job at a regional magazine, and eventually my holy grail—a job at a national magazine in New York City.

When I arrived at that job, I discovered that my boss frowned upon freelancing. But by then, I had trained my brain in a different way: I was convinced that my side hustle would always be more important, even at what felt like a dream job. So I adjusted my approach. I bought a wireless keyboard, which I connected to my phone, so that I could sneak out of the office, sit on a bench in a crowded part of Manhattan, and interview someone for another magazine while typing my notes onto an iPhone. I sometimes wrote under a pseudonym. I also started teaching writing, which I saw as a kind of invisible freelancing—my boss would never notice. Again, it worked: More experience meant more relationships, and more relationships meant more job opportunities.

As you read this, you may be thinking: *Wait, does "working your next job" just mean being a really bad employee?"*

The answer: yes and no. Let's take a step back.

The Side Hustler's Dilemma

Because I run a magazine about entrepreneurship, people like to tell me how their entrepreneurship journey began. A common story starts like this: "I was working at [insert big company here], and they disapproved of my side hustle, so I quit (or got fired)." Then the person's side hustle became a full hustle, and now they're more satisfied (and maybe even making more money) than they ever were before.

Recently, a woman named LaToya Westbrooks Keeling told me about working at a big bank and leaving when her superiors complained about a financial literacy and coaching company called Wealthly that she'd started on the side. What a stupid bank. What a big, dumb, stupid, shortsighted, stuck-in-the-past, shooting-itself-in-the-foot, unable-to-retain-its-top-talent, dedicated-to-mediocrity bank. This woman's program is now thriving, and her former employer doesn't have access to her, her ideas, her energy, or her drive. The bank seems intent on limiting itself to employees who think small. The bank seems to think that *it alone* should be the only career opportunity available to its employees—as if a job at a bank can inspire people to infinite greatness. That's implausible. No: impossible! The bank blew it because, like so many employers, it could not understand the limitless capacity of people who think big.

Anyone who is always discovering and creating and building is an entrepreneur and should be viewed as a highly valued employee. An entrepreneur doesn't have to own a company; it's simply someone with a creation mindset. An entrepreneur builds things for themselves, and they inspire others to do the same. An entrepreneur works at 150% capacity—and if that person is on your team and afforded the freedom to thrive, they'll give you 100% and keep 50% for themselves. If you are an employer, seek out and embrace those people, because they are your future. And if you're one of those people, you should refuse to be contained.

Are you working for someone else? Did they give you a guaranteed contract for life? No? Now you know your situation. The only lifelong contract you have is with yourself.

As evidence of this wisdom, I give you Richelle DeVoe.

DeVoe started her career in the nonprofit world, working on get-out-the-vote campaigns. Eventually, as she says, she decided it was time to make "a living wage." She decided to join the corporate world and found an opportunity to help scale a company's customer service department. Was she passionate about customer service? Not really. "I had heard that there were opportunities within this company to really grow," she told me. So she took it.

This was a good and bad decision. As it turns out, she hated customer service. But she wanted to be valuable for her company, so she started looking around to see what else she could learn. "I knew that I needed to develop skills for a job that I wanted, not the one I had," she said. She made a list of the subjects that excited her: marketing, storytelling, and psychology. How could that fit together? Then she heard that her company was doing customer insights research—that is, strategically interviewing customers (and noncustomers) about their needs and interests, so that the company could better serve them. "I didn't know where it would go, but I knew I wanted to learn more," she said. So in her spare time at work, DeVoe started listening to the interviews and learning more about the process.

She was fascinated by what she learned. There was an art and science to these interviews, and the insights they yielded were powerful. "I was hoping that I would be able to grow within the company, do marketing, and do insights research for the company itself," she said.

In an ideal world, the company would have recognized DeVoe's potential. My old boss Mike Elfland, an editor at one of the local newspapers I worked at, often summed up his management style with a baseball metaphor: "We don't want our best first baseman playing in the outfield." In other words, he wanted to run a fluid organization—identifying his team members' talents and then shifting their roles to maximize success. Credit to him, that's what he did. People moved around a lot. But most bosses aren't Elfand. Most bosses are like DeVoe's boss, and they're not interested in adapting. They're interested in *filling*—they have a role that needs filled, and they want a person to fill it, and they don't especially care if that person is better suited elsewhere. DeVoe recognized the limitations, and the company recognized that she'd be unhappy in her role. They parted ways.

Then she started her own consulting company offering a range of services, based on things she'd picked up in her previous few jobs—marketing, messaging, sales copy, customer insights research, and more. One client hired her for customer insights, and the person was so thrilled with the result that the client told friends, who also started hiring DeVoe just for customer insights. "This skill set that was originally only one tiny piece of what I offered in my own company became the thing that I was known for," DeVoe says. Eventually the consulting company Pen Name, which I mentioned earlier, made her an offer she couldn't refuse, and she joined its team—to head up their customer insights (the very thing she was interested in at her old company).

In short: DeVoe had a job she didn't like, then learned a new skill because it seemed interesting. She had no expectations of where this new skill would take her, but it ultimately defined the next phase of her career. DeVoe had worked her next job. Was she a bad employee in the process? Sure, maybe—she wasn't good at the thing she was hired to do. But instead of doing a half-assed job, she found a way to make herself more valuable. Her employer didn't recognize this, which was its own fault, so the company lost out on DeVoe's talents.

It doesn't always have to work out that way. I'm a prime example of how working your next job can actually *benefit* your employer.

Back in 2011, I was hired as an editor at *Fast Company*. My job was to edit stories in the print magazine. Then *Fast Company* created a video team—and although nobody asked me to join, I volunteered. It seemed like a good skill to have, and I imagined it might create new opportunities for me. Maybe someone would offer me a TV show!

As it turns out, nobody offered me a TV show. However, I became good on camera and starred in two regular video series for *Fast Company*. I drove viewership and new sponsors, which was valuable to my employer. Eventually I left that job. Because of this new skill set I'd learned, I felt emboldened to launch a podcast and pursue speaking opportunities onstage. This became a zigzag payoff: Years later, when I was applying to be editor in chief of *Entrepreneur,* one of the reasons the president and CEO liked me was that I could be a good speaker and advocate for the brand.

In short, when I worked my next job, I learned a new skill and helped my company. I also set myself up for an opportunity years later that I could have never anticipated or planned for.

So let's ask the question again: *Wait, does "working your next job" just mean being a really bad employee?* Now you see why the answer is yes and no. When you work your next job, you become more valuable to your company—and if your employer recognizes and benefits from that, then they're lucky to get more of you than they'd have otherwise gotten. If they don't recognize it, then oh well—it's their loss, and you've set yourself up for future success.

Imagine standing at the intersection of one thousand roads. You don't know where they'll all go, but you do know that they they're twisty and winding, and some lead to fantastic success. At the start of our careers, however, 999 of these roads are closed to us. We just go down one of them—and as we do, we have a choice to make. We can keep going down that one road, hoping we don't hit a roadblock, or we can actively work to open more of these roads. Where will they go? It's unpredictable. But the more roads we open, the more pathways to success we create. This way, unpredictability becomes its own kind of opportunity.

Consider:

For me, one of these new roads was video. It led, rather unexpectedly, to me launching a podcast and running a magazine.

For DeVoe, one of these new roads was customer insights research. It led, rather unexpectedly, to her joining a company as its head of customer insights research.

DeVoe joined Pen Name, which is run by old friends of mine.

When I needed help growing my podcast, I hired my friends. They put DeVoe on the job. She learned my audience's needs in a way I never could, and she delivered insights that transformed my understanding of my show, my message, and myself.

When you work your next job, you never know what will happen. But I can guarantee this: You will make yourself more adaptable.

PART 3

New
Normal

The panic (Phase 1) has passed, and we've primed ourselves to adapt (Phase 2) to our new challenges and opportunities. Now it's time for Phase 3—to steady our legs and make use of what we've got, while remaining clear-eyed about what we know and what we don't (yet).

This is about creating a "new normal." But this doesn't mean a life without new changes. And it's not as easy as it sounds. After feeling disrupted by change, we will be desperate for something familiar and predictable. We will want to create new rules and stick to them, believing that, just like in the old days, we knew exactly what we needed and exactly how to get it. We'll be tempted to skip the hard stuff—which is to say, things will go wrong and we'll feel defeated, and we may not challenge ourselves as much as we should.

To give you a sense of the difficulties ahead, I want to first tell you a cautionary tale. It's one in which we all collectively jumped to conclusions, desperate for simple answers to complex problems, so that we could easily understand what felt like a New Normal.

I'm talking about the Russian interference in America's 2016 presidential election—a moment in which, regardless of political position, everyone seemed to agree that something about this felt new, and that our old expectations had been upended. Change had come to a foundational element of America. And so politicians and media pundits used one word repeatedly to describe what happened: *unprecedented.* But was it?

The hacking, the release of emails, the deployment of Twitter trolls, the spread of misinformation—all of it was labeled unprecedented. They used that word on cable news and in congressional hearings. But was it, in fact, *unprecedented*? David Shimer didn't think so; he's an associate fellow at Yale University, and was concerned about the use of this word. "To me, that's dangerous," he said. "If you treat something as unprecedented, what you're saying is there's no history behind it. What you're saying is it's never happened before, and that makes it much easier to create rumors, myths, and even lies about a subject."

If something is totally new and unprecedented, then we can reasonably assume it has a new and simple cause. If I wake up and discover that my face has turned lime green, which would be an unprecedented problem for me, then I'd think: *What did I do yesterday? Did I eat something I'd never eaten before, or touch something I'd never touched before?* New cause, new effect. The same seemed true for Russia's interference: Because people thought it was unprecedented, they tried to pinpoint new and active causes. The general conclusion was that this is social media's fault. Facebook became the villain of the story.

But to understand just how un-unprecedented Russia's actions were, Shimer spoke to more than 130 former officials, including eight former CIA directors and a former KGB general, and then wrote a book called *Rigged: America, Russia, and One Hundred Years of Covert Electoral Interference.* In it, he details a full century of Russia running the exact same playbook: Use the newest technologies of the time to exacerbate existing tensions in American society. Russia did it with newspapers in the 1920s, radio in the 1940s, TV in the 1950s, and more. In 1960, at the United Nations General Assembly, Russia even sent a racist letter to some African and Asian delegations and pretended it came from the Ku Klux Klan.

When this letter was read aloud at the assembly, it caused America great embarrassment. Russian Twitter bots in 2016 were just a new form of an old plan. With this context, Russia's modern actions weren't unprecedented. They were in fact *very precedented.*

This has major implications for how we even begin to understand the problem we face. If you believe that Russia's actions were "unprecedented," then it's easy to believe that social media is the culprit. That in turn means that the solution lies in regulating or otherwise controlling the reach and use of social media. But once you see that Russia's playbook predates social media, you can see that social media solutions alone cannot actually fix the larger problem. That means we need to think bigger and more creatively. "If Russia is seeking to tear down our democracy, which it is, then we need to renew our democracy both at home and abroad," Shimer told me. That means securing our election infrastructure, citizens becoming more well informed and less gullible, investment in public education and institutions, renewed leadership abroad, and more. This is hard, complex stuff. And we'll never even begin attempting it if we stick with a simplified narrative.

Why am I telling you about this now? It's not to be political. It's because this is a lesson for us all, as we enter the New Normal phase of change.

First, let this serve as an important warning about oversimplifying change. As we return to some level of comfort after change, we want to feel a sense of understanding and competency. We want to find new solutions and build upon them. And as we do this, we'll be tempted to simplify—to turn complex issues into something basic, and make decisions based on our more limited understanding of a situation. (Remember our exercise about what year Gandhi was born in? We cannot narrow our bands!)

As we do this, we'll also be tempted to forget the past. We'll see a new opportunity or challenge, and we'll ignore or lack curiosity about whatever came before it. But we cannot truly address a problem if we don't know where it came from—and that's just as true on a national level as it is on a personal level.

When we're grappling with change, whether it's good or bad, the solution is almost surely more complex than we'd like to think it is. As we enter New Normal, let's hold on to the humbleness we learned during Panic and Adaptation. We do not know everything. We cannot grab one piece of information—one small part of a larger change—and believe that it alone can guide us.

Almost nothing is unprecedented. Our New Normal will one day be an Old Normal, replaced by yet another New Normal. We are not arriving at a destination. We're simply planting our feet on the ground, until it's time to jump again.

chapter 9

Treat Failure as Data

As we begin our journey into the New Normal, let's start with that first word: *new*.

What does it mean to try something new? For many people, it means risk and the potential of failure. That's why, in the world of business, you'll often hear this claim: *Nine out of ten new businesses fail.*

I'm asked about this statistic all the time. It doesn't matter if you plan to start a business or not—that number still sounds terrifying. It seems like proof that most new ideas are bad, and that most people who chase their dreams will regret it. It suggests that you should stay put, like a prairie dog in its hole, because risk is not rewarded.

Don't believe any of that. The statistic is wrong—by the numbers, and more important by its definition of *fail.* Once you see *how* it's wrong, you'll also start to see the concept of "new" itself differently.

First, the facts: About half of businesses survive their first four years, according to the U.S. Census Bureau. Does that mean the other half failed? No. At the time that they closed, about a third of those businesses were successful. "It appears that many owners may have executed a planned exit strategy, closed a business without excess debt, sold a viable business, or retired from the work force," the study says. In other words: Just because a business ends, that doesn't mean it ends badly.

It's unsurprising that we'd conflate these ideas, though. We have a collective problem with the concepts of *success* and *failure*—so let's dig into what's going on there for a moment before returning to the idea of business failure.

"We've defined success at a societal level so narrowly," says Harvard professor Todd Rose. He spoke with an *Entrepreneur* colleague of mine for a story we ran about the skilled-trade labor shortage in America. Stable, well-paying jobs as electricians and plumbers are going unfilled, because so many people were raised to believe that college and subsequent white-collar jobs are the only true definition of success. "What worries me," Rose said in the story, "is that many people are forgoing the kind of training that would actually lead to a more secure and fulfilling life in order to play a game they don't even want to play but think they have to."

What underlies this problem? Rose has an interesting way to illuminate it. In addition to his work at Harvard, he's also the cofounder of Populace, a social impact think tank, and his group did a study of how Americans view their ideal lives. Most respondents said they value relationships and fulfillment over fame and money. But when asked if other people share their views, most respondents said no. They believed that most Americans are the opposite of them, and value fame and money over relationships and fulfillment.

That's a remarkable disconnect! Most Americans have the same exact values, but they also believe that they are *alone* in these values. They are literally alone together, living in the majority while believing they're in the minority. As a result, Rose says, people tend to stay quiet about their own values—which allows a smaller number of loud voices, like pundits and TV stars and a small group of "experts," to define *success* and *failure* for us.

This is problematic. When we cannot define success for ourselves, we will struggle against unattainable goals—or perhaps never try something new at all.

Here's a small but telling example. Whenever I speak with aspiring podcasters, they always ask a version of this question: "How many downloads do I need to be successful?" Here's what they're really saying: *Please tell me what success looks like, so I can decide if I can achieve that or not.* But there is no answer to this! There is no single way to be a "successful" podcaster. Sure, Tim Ferriss gets hundreds of millions of downloads, which means his show earns him gobs of money, and that is one obvious way to measure success. But success can take many other forms. Some podcasters have no interest in reaching millions of people; they just want to reach the *right* people. For example, my friends Hanna Lee and Michael Anstendig run a PR agency that's focused on the hospitality and travel industry, and I helped them start a podcast, Hospitality Forward, about how these industries can earn media attention. Their episodes only get hundreds of listens—but about two months after launching, a gin distillery heard the show, reached out, and hired them to do PR work. More connections followed. Listeners began sharing how the show helped their business. To my friends, that made the podcast a success.

Is something a success or failure? That depends on how you measure up against *your* goal, not someone else's. Never ask what success looks like. It looks like whatever you want.

With that understanding, let's now return to that bogus statistic: *Nine out of ten new businesses fail.*

Even if the stat were true, we would still need to define the word *fail.* If a business truly does fail—if it ran out of money, laid off its staff, and totally crashed and burned—is that a failure? Maybe . . . but maybe not! Great businesses have been built out of the lessons from failed ones. YouTube began as a failed dating site; Twitter began as a failed podcast platform called Odeo; Instagram began as a failed app to help plan meetups called Burbn.

This is not just true for companies. The most successful people in the world have told me that they attribute their successes to their failures. Tennis champion Maria Sharapova said she gets frustrated when people think she's just innately good at things; the peak of her career came as a result of decades of failure, she says, and it taught her to align with people who could navigate those downsides along with her. "I hired people I could lose with—who I'd be comfortable losing with—because they're who would give me the best support," she told me. "If they're people you'd want to be with when you lose, then I'm sure you'll be able to celebrate well with them." Meanwhile, Michael Dell, the billionaire founder of Dell Technologies, literally keeps mementos in his office from his company's past failures, because they represent hard-earned lessons to him. "That painful lesson helped us develop a tremendous capability that propelled us way further than we'd ever imagined," he told me.

To say that something *failed*, simply because it *stopped* or *changed*, is to dangerously limit our view of the world. Even if 9 out of 10 businesses fail, we could not say that 9 out of 10 *entrepreneurs* fail.

I know this can sound trite. There's a wonderful quote attributed to IBM founding chairman Thomas J. Watson that goes, "If you want to succeed, double your failure rate." But Watson probably didn't say that *while* he was failing. Failure is only glorified in retrospect.

So instead of looking at the past, let's zoom in on the present—when change is here, the old normal is gone, the New Normal has not yet been established, and failure feels very possible and very final. What do you do next?

Here's the answer: You stop thinking of failure as failure, and you start thinking of it as data.

To see that in action, let's go shopping.

First to Failure, First to Solutions

Back in 2013, before I had little kids who constantly burst into my bathroom, I really enjoyed listening to podcasts in the shower. One day I went onto Amazon searching for a low-cost, waterproof, Bluetooth-enabled, rechargeable speaker. I assumed I'd find many options. Instead, there was only one: It was a black-and-green blob of a speaker called Hipe. Was that the brand name, or the model? The customer reviewers didn't seem to know, but they all said some version of the same thing: The speaker works as advertised, and if you have questions, some guy named Sam is responsive by email.

I've spent $69.99 on worse. I bought it right away.

The speaker worked as advertised, but I had a question about connectivity. I emailed Hipe, and, sure enough, Sam replied. He wrote, "This is the answer I got from China, does this help at all?" Then he pasted a chunk of broken-English text that, after some parsing, was, in fact, helpful. But now Hipe made even less sense. Why is this company copy-and-pasting from "China"? Who is behind all this? I googled around and connected Hipe to a New Jersey company called C&A Marketing, then emailed Sam to ask how the two were related.

His reply, in full: " 🙂 "

Now I *needed* to know what was going on here! I badgered. I pled. I finally talked Sam into meeting with me, and we set a date, but then he quickly retracted and put me in touch with a marketing guy, who put me in touch with a publicist, who invited me to a photography trade show in Manhattan called PhotoPlus and gave me these instructions: Come to the Polaroid stand and ask for Chaim.

I mean, how could I *not*?

At the appointed time, I did as I was told. That's how I met Chaim Piekarski, an Orthodox Jewish man with a wispy red beard who seemed delighted at my confusion. He talked in riddles about how many products he has, and how he knew exactly what I wanted as a consumer, which is why he built that waterproof speaker with all the right features. "My wife and kids don't buy anything for the house," he told me. "Whenever they buy something, they're always afraid I'm going to come home and say, 'You know, I sell that.'"

I felt like I was talking to Willy Wonka. None of it made sense. I asked to visit his warehouse in New Jersey, figuring that I'd finally get some concrete answers there (and then I could write about it for *Fast Company,* where I worked at the time). Piekarski agreed. A few weeks later, he walked me around a 150,000-square-foot space piled high with boxes of random products. Wi-Fi boosters here, flashlights there. Piekarski seemed amused and dismissive of each one. When we passed a shipment of egg cookers, he said, "There's nothing innovative about it. You like cooked eggs!"

Then I finally learned where all of this had come from. It was the result of a series of failures.

Piekarski started out in the camera film business. But in 2001, as digital cameras destroyed his sales, he sold it off and partnered with a onetime competitor. Two years later, the men unveiled C&A Marketing and sold digital cameras. This wasn't a safe industry, either; smartphones were about to disrupt the marketplace. In 2008, C&A began making lenses and other camera accessories, and then expanded out to consumer electronics.

That's when Piekarski had his breakthrough insight. He was selling most of his wares through Amazon, and he realized that Amazon was far more than just a sales platform. It was actually a giant, free, untapped research-and-development lab. He could look at other companies' popular product reviews to see what consumers liked—and more important, what they did not. Maybe, for example, they liked a waterproof speaker, but kept saying they wished it had rechargeable batteries. No problem: Piekarski could then contract with a manufacturer in China, do a small run of this upgraded product, sell it under a totally meaningless brand name (like Hipe), and see what happens. If it sells well, he'd make more. If not, he'd discontinue it and try something else.

Piekarski has systematized this to a hilarious degree. He led me into a room full of cubicles, all occupied by bearded, yarmulke-wearing men in crisp white shirts. (That's Piekarski's network, after all. At the time, about half of C&A Marketing's 150-person staff was Orthodox, though one buyer was not; he was Italian. Piekarski let that guy work from home.) One of the men in this room is Sam Kain, the man who originally replied to my email. These men all oversee a particular product category, and they spend part of their days scouring online reviews of existing products—looking for an opportunity to create a new, slightly better version based on what people say they want.

When I met Piekarski in 2013, C&A Marketing was a nine-figure business (he wouldn't be more specific) that was growing 30% annually. Today it's called C+A Global, and is among the world's largest third-party platform sellers on Amazon and other retailers. It has offices in New Jersey, London, and China, and has gobbled up distressed brands that it can iterate on. Piekarski owns and operates RitzCamera.com, for example, as well as SkyMall, that catalog you used to find on airplanes.

As I've watched this company grow, I often think back to Piekarski's journey. He began in the camera film business, which became practically obsolete, and some might have called that a failure. But Piekarski did not call it a failure; his work in the film industry helped him see where consumers were going next, and so he built a digital camera business that thrived for a handful of years. Then he had a front-row seat for *that* industry's disruption—which meant he could spot his consumers' new and evolving needs, then shift to meet them, and ultimately develop a deep and sophisticated understanding of the world's most powerful e-commerce platform. Seen one way, sure, Piekarski kept chasing failed business models. But seen another way, Piekarski was getting real-time data faster than anyone else, and was using it to stay ahead of his competition.

This is how failure can become data. If you "fail," it happens because you're further into the storm than other people are. You're seeing change first—which means you have insights that others do not. That can be a powerful position if you're willing to recognize it.

And how do you recognize it? You begin by stepping back from every moment of perceived failure, as well as from every time you feel disrupted by the forces of change, and you ask yourself: *What did I just learn that I didn't know before, and that other people may still not have learned?*

It is not an easy question. But after you drain the emotion out of any difficult or embarrassing moment, that question can help give your experience a new purpose. It is true whether your job or company is disrupted, or your entire life is. To see this play out in the extreme, I talked to a guy who reached the pinnacle of his career—and then had it crash down around him in every possible way.

Will It Help Me or Hurt Me?

Not long ago, I was talking to eleven-time NBA All-Star Chris Bosh. He won two championships and an Olympic gold medal, but he's suffered many losses, too. I told him about my theory that failure is data. I wanted to know if he agreed with it.

"Absolutely," he said. Then he told me about the 2011 NBA Finals. That was the first year that he, LeBron James, and Dwyane Wade had teamed up on the Miami Heat, which was an earth-shaking move in the world of basketball. Expectations for success were unmeasurable. The Heat made it to the finals, but then, to almost everyone's surprise, the team lost to the considerably less flashy Dallas Mavericks. "It was just crushing," Bosh said. He cried on national TV, which he was embarrassed about. But ultimately, he and his teammates stepped back and asked themselves a version of that question: *What did I just learn that I didn't know before, and that other people may still not have learned?* The answer, they realized, was the need for emotional steadiness. Whenever the Heat won a game in that finals series, they were ecstatic. Whenever they lost, they were crushed. Their highs were too high, and their lows were too low. The Mavs stayed right in the middle, which helped them win. "We took it as a data point," Bosh told me. And they won the next year.

This wasn't the only reason I wanted to talk with Bosh. Sure, he won and lost on the court—but that's what players are *supposed* to do. The ups and downs of the NBA are not comparable to most people's lives or professions. But what happened to Bosh *next* is very human and relatable. Bosh developed blood clots, and in 2016, a doctor determined that he could no longer play basketball. So just like that, Bosh's career was over. He'd worked with a singular focus for most of his life, with the goal of having a long and successful career in the NBA—and then every goal and aspiration he had was torn away from him, unable to be fulfilled. He had nothing.

This isn't a *failure,* per se. It was hardly his fault. But then again, change is rarely our fault. It is rarely something we conjure ourselves. But we alone must deal with the repercussions of it, which can often feel a lot like failure—if not a failure of our own making, then at least the failure of our expectations. And . . . then what?

That's the bigger question I had for Bosh. Could failure be data in his *life,* and not just in a high-stakes basketball game?

Here, again, Bosh said yes.

After Bosh's blood clots, he did what you might expect: He spent a lot of time figuring out how to get back into basketball. Maybe there was some medical treatment, or some new diagnosis, that could make this all go away? Once those paths were exhausted, he felt lost. He had always read a lot of self-help books. "I remember all those books saying, like, 'Just do what you love,'" he told me. "And I was like, 'Yeah, OK, easier said than done. Now I'm in this position and I have to *find* what I love.'"

He'd long been interested in music and books, so he started to explore that. Maybe he could write something? "I just kept doing it," he told me. "Did it make sense at the time? No. It was very foggy. But I just continued. And I feel that, in doing those things, and staying with it, things just started kind of materializing." A small idea turned into a book called *Letters to a Young Athlete,* which is a collection of advice aimed at young and aspiring athletes like he once was.

"I came to the realization that, OK, I have a choice: Is this going to help me, or is it going to hurt me?" he said. "I choose that it is going to help me. And it's going to propel me. You know, I may be down right now. I may be out. But this situation is going to propel me to where I need to go in the future, because what other option do you have? That's one of the main lessons that I learned as an athlete, when pursuing championships and greatness: It's just not going to be handed over to you. You're going to have obstacles and challenges. You're going to have to get over them. So attack it with enthusiasm. I eventually got to the point where I joke: In writing a book about obstacles, I had to get over obstacles writing the book."

Things end. When Bosh lost his career, his time in the NBA ended. When someone opens a small business, and it closes within four years, that also ended. But of course, no ending is final. Bosh, like the business owner, did not cease to exist after one phase of his career concluded. These people had more journey to travel, and more growth to explore. So they began with the information—the data!—that they had available to them. Something from before helped them orient to now. For Bosh, he expanded upon other passions like music and reading—but even more so, he reframed what he'd learned in sports, about how every pursuit has challenges that must be met. He didn't fully appreciate the power of this perspective until he was faced with a life-altering experience. That is data. The data is what will move him ahead.

Now, a personal note about all this:

Back in 2010, more than a decade before the conversation with Bosh that I just described to you, I was a junior editor at *Men's Health*. A publicist emailed me with an invitation . . . for my boss. Was I his secretary? No. This was insulting. But the email was intriguing. The publicist was inviting my boss to have dinner with Bosh, who at the time had just left the Toronto Raptors and was heading to the Miami Heat. I'd been a Heat fan since childhood. So when I shared it with my boss, I said, "If you can't make it, I'd be happy to go!"

"Go," my boss said. "I'm busy that night."

The publicist was displeased. I was just some kid, not the impressive magazine editor she'd hoped to score. But she was stuck, unable to rescind the invite. I went.

The dinner was at a fancy steakhouse in Manhattan. It was me, Bosh, a major fashion designer, a major TV producer, Bosh's wife, Adrienne, and some of her friends. I was deeply, comically out of place among these far wealthier, more successful people, who chatted about places I'd never seen and things I'd never afforded. But I chimed in whenever I could, and everyone, Bosh included, was gracious and welcoming. At the end of the dinner, we all agreed to stay in touch—though, of course, I never heard from any of them again.

Was this a successful dinner, or a failure? The case for failure: I was unwanted (by the publicist, at least), and I failed to make much of an impression on these big shots around the table. The case for success: I had dinner with the future star of my favorite team, and I also learned what it looked and felt like to be sitting at a powerful table, which could help me feel more comfortable in a setting like this in the future. I chose then to think of it as a success. I still do. I felt like I'd snuck through a secret door.

Life went on. Bosh helped Miami win two championships, and then his NBA career ended. I rose in magazines, and eventually became the boss of one. When Bosh and I reconnected in 2021, to talk about everything you just read, I began by reminding him of the dinner we had eleven years earlier.

"That's dope, man," he said to me. "Junior writer to the lead man. That's what's up."

"That's what we work for, isn't it?" I said.

"Absolutely," he said. "We don't work to be average."

That's exceptionally true. We work to be extraordinary. Along the way, we will feel out of place, struggle to grow, make hard decisions, and face massive setbacks. We will lose. We will fail. We will experience things that feel final. But this, too, is why we work: It's so we build a stable foundation upon which we can be extraordinary in ways we may never have imagined.

Like me back at that 2010 dinner, and like all of us at some point, Bosh is now putting himself in new and uncomfortable situations. He also knows the purpose of it: When you work hard enough, and treat failure like data, you stop being the kid at the table who doesn't belong.

That is what *new* means.

Now let's talk about what's "normal."

chapter 10

Build a Bridge of Familiarity

You've surely heard the phrase "You can't have your cake and eat it, too." It's a figure of speech meant to describe someone who wants two contradictory things—for example, if someone wants a happy monogamous marriage, but this person is also sleeping with their neighbor, then they are trying to have their cake and eat it, too. The phrase always bothered me because the syntax doesn't make sense. If I have a cake . . . well, why can't I eat it, too? Have cake, eat cake: That seems like a logical progression of events! But history clears up the confusion. The phrase as we know it is, in fact, a reversal of the original phrase. It dates to the 1500s and went roughly like this: "You can't eat your cake and have it, too." That is true. You cannot eat a cake, and then still have a cake. When you eat it, it's gone.

Our relationship with change is exactly like this. We like new things, but we don't want to lose our old things. We want it both ways—we want to eat endless cake. And you know what? With the right kind of thinking, we can.

We need to give ourselves *new* and *old* at the same time. I call this the Bridge of Familiarity: It's a matter of identifying parts of our old experience that do not change, and then using them to reframe the new opportunity in front of us. Your boss asks you to do part of your job differently, and it's frustrating until you realize how it helps your original goals. You move across the country, and feel out of place until you discover the parts of your new city that resemble your old one. You're afraid to leave a job you're unhappy in, until you identify how the skills you built there can be used in totally new ways. Your kids start using a new technology, and it seems like it's harming them until you realize they're doing exactly what you did as a kid.

Oftentimes, the Bridge of Familiarity is not easy to find. It's why, when we're presented with something new, we often panic.

Throughout this book, I've already detailed many common things that were once considered terrifying or scandalous. But to show you the power of familiarity, let's start with one thing that *wasn't* considered all that scary at first. It was one of the most transformative inventions of all: electricity.

Here's some quick electricity history—the first part of which you may know, but the second part of which is often ignored by the history books. Thomas Edison built the first electric generator in New York in 1882. He championed a form of electricity called direct current, but his competitors George Westinghouse and Nikola Tesla invested in a more versatile form called alternating current, and so Edison tried to turn public opinion against alternating current by claiming that it was uncontrollable and deadly (and even arranging to have the first-ever prisoner execution via electric chair be powered by a Westinghouse machine). This became known as the "war of the currents," and things got ugly. But ultimately, he lost: Edison's direct current still has uses today, but our homes and offices are primarily powered by alternating current.

Now here's what is often ignored about this story: Despite Edison's fearmongering, most people did not consider electricity to be controversial. This would seem surprising, considering that electricity is certainly more consequential than once-maligned inventions like teddy bears and comic books. Electricity lit up the night. It transformed our homes. It paved the way for nearly every major convenience and innovation that followed—radio, television, air-conditioning, computers. It was perhaps the greatest agent of change the world has ever seen.

So why were people not afraid? Because in those early days, electricity was not viewed as some wild force poised to transform the world. It was primarily known for doing one thing—and that was bringing light into people's homes. "It wasn't like light was a new experience," Jill Jonnes, a historian and the author of the book *Empires of Light,* told me. "It's just that this light was a superior light, and far more convenient and actually less dangerous."

Prior to the 1880s, lighting a home meant lighting a flame. Gas pipes were fed through people's walls, where they'd fuel little gas-powered lamps. But that was dangerous. If a flame went out without someone realizing it, gas would continue to seep into a home—and people could die of gas poisoning. Electricity eliminated that danger.

In other words, electricity wasn't seen as delivering something new. It was delivering something *old* in a *new way.* It was a safer version of something people already had. That's why it was so easily embraced. *Lighting* was electricity's Bridge of Familiarity.

But electricity was a bit of a fluke. Change doesn't often come with a built-in bridge. In fact, it's often the opposite: When innovators release something new into the world, they are so convinced by their genius that they forget to explain it, or they make no effort to earn people's trust and comfort.

What Never Changes

Before laying out how to build your own Bridge of Familiarity, let's first back up a moment to consider this: We tend to believe that if something looks different, it *is* different.

Imagine, for example, that you time-traveled back to the 1950s and asked someone, "What does community look like to you?" They might say that it looks like bowling leagues or pasta dinners at church. Then ask, "What does communication look like to you?" They might say it looks like long, handwritten letters or lengthy telephone calls.

Now listen to the older generation today, as they watch young people text instead of call, or play Fortnite with friends when there's no time to see them in person. The older person will lament: *Community is gone! Communication is gone!*

Earlier in this book, we discussed the difference between our *what* and our *why*. When people of an older generation bemoan a younger generation's actions, they're doing the same thing: They confuse *what* kids do with *why* they do it. And in this case, the *why* is something that's core to humanity—a trait that's deeply embedded in us, like building community and connecting with others. The *what* is simply how any single generation expresses this core trait, based on the resources available to them. As we already know, *whats* will always change. Bowling leagues were fun for a time, until they became viewed as an activity for grandpa. Phone calls are enjoyable sometimes. They were also once the only way to contact someone quickly, but now we do things differently. Community and communication are expressed in different ways, but that doesn't mean community and communication are gone! Just because something looks different, that doesn't mean it is different.

This may sound simple and silly—just the grumblings of old people who don't understand new technology. But it's more than that. It's a critical insight into how we think as a group, and how much we crave familiarity. We don't want radical new ways of doing things; that feels disorienting and scary. But we *do* like improvements in our lives! We like new things, so long as they fit snugly beside our old things.

Again, it's the Bridge of Familiarity. On an individual level, or on a societal level, this bridge must be built if we (and others!) are to ever truly embrace change.

Now, with that in mind, let's talk about cars.

A New Version of an Old Thing

Here's the history of cars that most people know: *Henry Ford.*

That's it. That's the history. Ford wasn't the first guy to make a car, but he manufactured cars with such scale and efficiency that, for the first time, this transformational new vehicle was affordable and accessible to all. The Model T began rolling off the production line in 1908 and went straight into the driveway of every home in America, and this has become the automobile's origin story. Victory for Ford! The end.

But that's not actually the story, according to Imes Chiu, whose years of doctoral research and examination of primary sources informed her book about the history of the car called *The Evolution from Horse to Automobile.*

Ford did revolutionize manufacturing, but he didn't actually make the cheapest cars. As early as 1898, cars were selling for $600—cheaper than the Model T would eventually be. Also, a market for used cars appeared almost immediately. So even if you couldn't afford a new car, you could grab an old one.

But most people didn't, notes Brian Ladd in his book *Autophobia: Love and Hate in the Automotive Age.* Cars became known as "devil wagons." At the dawn of the auto age, English philosopher C. E. M. Joad wrote that "motoring is one of the most contemptible soul-destroying and devitalizing pursuits that the ill-fortune of misguided humanity has ever imposed upon its credulity." When cars would drive by, people on the side of streets started throwing rocks at them. Oftentimes, bystanders would yell, "Get a horse!" Drivers had to start arming themselves with guns, in case mobs seized upon them. Laws were passed to limit or outlaw cars on streets entirely.

By 1902, eight years before Ford came along, the nascent car industry realized it had a problem, as Chiu reports. Why weren't people excited to drive this revolutionary new technology? Eventually, the industry realized the problem: It was talking about cars all wrong.

The earliest automobile advertisements presented the car as a radically new thing. Its message was basically: *Ditch your horse!* The auto industry believed that its cars were superior to horses, and it assumed everyone would agree.

People didn't appreciate that. They liked their horses. The horses were family! And they didn't want these know-it-all industry people—the late-1800s version of Silicon Valley tech bros—telling them to radically alter their lives.

Then the car industry took a different approach. Instead of presenting cars as a replacement to the horse, it talked about cars as *a better horse.*

One early ad described a car this way: "As strong as a giant, and sensitive and spirited as a thoroughbred horse." A 1903 Oldsmobile ad compared the steering wheel to a pair of reins and suggested that the vehicle's controls required the same intuitive skill as directing the horse. One auto manufacturer at the time claimed that the horse head replica attached to the front of its car functioned as an external gas tank. "You have these efforts to mimic an old, established technology, take some of the features in it and incorporate it into this radically new controversial technology, in order to assist the public to make this conceptual shift," Chiu told me.

The word *horsepower* also gained popularity during this time. Advertisements in the early 1900s, like the ones from the Autocar Company in

1905, compare driving its Type XI with the same simplicity as horse driving; the left and right grips control the throttle and spark "simple as a pair of reins." It's also why manufacturers named their cars after horses—a legacy that was carried on with the likes of the Dodge Colt, and Ford's Mustang and Bronco.

This is what really laid the groundwork for Ford's success, according to Chiu. The horse was a car's Bridge of Familiarity. Once people thought of the car as a new version of an old thing, they were primed to buy into Ford's commercial operation.

Decades later, the story would repeat with another revolutionary mode of transportation—though this one would take us up and down.

Humanizing Innovation

For a very long time, elevators were a terrible idea: It was literally a box attached to a rope, which would carry miners up and down a shaft. The rope often snapped, sending everyone plummeting to their death. By the 1830s, these things were upgraded and started to be installed in buildings. The box was a little sturdier; the rope was a little stronger. But there were still many ways it might murder you. The elevator might fall while you were in it. Or, *you* might fall without the elevator—because sometimes you'd be waiting for an elevator, the doors would open as if it had arrived, and then you'd absentmindedly step forward, discover with horror that the elevator *hadn't* arrived, and now you were hurtling downward. Or, you might try to enter or exit the elevator when it would abruptly jerk up or down and crush you.

By the 1850s, a series of innovations began fixing these problems. The most transformative came from Elisha Otis, who invented a new safety brake: If the rope broke and an elevator started to plummet, steel pawls would spring out from the crossbar at the top of the car, catch on to rachets in the guide rails, and save everyone's lives. (Otis's name is still the industry standard today: Look closely in the next elevator you're in, and you'll likely see it's made by the Otis Elevator Company.) As the device became safer, more people trusted it. But they didn't need to trust the *machine*. They trusted the human inside—because for nearly a century, the elevator had an operator.

If you've ever seen an elevator operator today, you've seen the human equivalent of a tonsil: It's a person doing a job that doesn't really need doing. Maybe they open the door for you. Maybe they press the floor button you request. But their job could easily be done by a machine. This was not true from 1860 to 1950, when elevator operators literally moved the elevator up and down by first pulling a rope, then by turning a crank, and finally by pushing a button.

Elevator operators were a source of comfort. When you stepped into this box, you knew you were in an experienced person's hands. But they were also a nuisance. Operator unions would go on strike, stranding building occupants wherever they were. (In 1943, for example, 250 elevator operators abruptly left their posts in the middle of the day around Rockefeller Center in Manhattan, trapping an estimated 28,000 people.) Even when they *were* working, the operators often clocked out at 5 p.m.—meaning that you could miss the last elevator of the day, the way you might miss a train today. After that, you were taking the stairs.

As time went on and technology improved, the elevator operator became less of a necessity. In the early 1950s, elevator manufacturers had a solution they thought the public would love: *fully automatic elevators!* Just tell the machine where you want to go, and it'll take you there—no operator required. This meant no more delays and strandings, and buildings would no longer need to employ operators. It seemed like an easy win for everyone (except the operators) . . . until people actually faced the prospect of stepping into one of these elevators themselves.

Then they started asking themselves: *Do you know what the elevator thinks?*

That was actually the headline of a column in *The Courier-Journal* of Louisville, Kentucky, in 1957. The writer pondered this: " *'The door has been taught to think,' say the elevator people. 'If the door touches any object in the doorway, it immediately withdraws.' That is what the elevator people THINK the door thinks. You know what I think the door thinks? I think it thinks: 'Getcha this time! SNAP!'* "

In short, people were freaked out. An unmanned elevator was unlike anything else we normally experience. Where else do you walk into a closed box with no windows and no human operator, and it physically moves you somewhere? "If they work really well, you can barely feel them move. This is all magic," said Lee Gray, a professor of architectural history at the University of North Carolina at Charlotte, when I asked him about this. "Well, it's kind of comforting if someone's there to take over if the magic suddenly doesn't work."

The elevator operators' union was of course also opposed to this new technology. It replaced their jobs! That's why they took advantage of people's discomfort, stoking as much fear as possible. They claimed that automatic elevators weren't safe, and that there were five times more accidents in automatic elevators. They also said automatic elevators would lead to more crime, which was an idea the press picked up on. In 1953, the *Chicago Daily News* reported that the local union president "said assaults, robberies, and even murders that have taken place in apartment houses and in their vestibules could have been prevented if elevators in the buildings were manned by operators."

Here it is—an exact replay of what happened with cars. Inventors assume that their new thing has obvious benefits, and so they happily suggest that this new thing replace everyone's old thing. Cars would replace horses, and automatic elevators would replace elevator operators.

In both cases, people became deeply uncomfortable. They began clinging to the thing they knew, even if it was inferior or inefficient.

What did the elevator industry do in response? Here, history also repeats—because the industry built a Bridge of Familiarity. You can still find it in some elevators today. Manufacturers began installing a soothing female voice into the elevator, who would make basic announcements:

Going up.

Going down.

And so on.

This (along with some hefty marketing) did the job. It gave the terrifying, faceless machine a dash of humanity. It made travelers feel like somewhere, somehow, a human being was involved in their safety. So they went along for the ride.

How Three Becomes Four

Our world looked radically different before the car and the elevator. Roads were mixed spaces filled with people and animals and play and commerce. Buildings were rarely more than six stories tall, and the poor lived on top. (That way, the rich enjoyed the conveniences of a lower floor.) After both inventions took hold, the world reoriented. Our streets became arteries for automobiles; our skies became inhabited by the wealthy.

This is the power of the Bridge of Familiarity: It can literally change everything.

If you are an entrepreneur or leader, and you are in the position of introducing change to other people, then the Bridge of Familiarity has a more obvious application to you. Your job isn't just to create new things— it's also to create the bridge that leads to your new thing, so that the people you're working with, or the customers you're trying to entice, can more readily walk across it. Innovators often forget to do this; they're understandably so convinced of the brilliance of their innovation that they forget how foreign it may be to others. The result is backlash.

But the Bridge of Familiarity can also be a helpful tactic for any individual who grapples with change. That's because we can build this bridge ourselves, by first identifying the things we know, and then figuring out what parts of them come along for the journey.

I have an exercise to help. A bridge takes us from *here* to *there,* so we're going to begin with *here*—with ourselves.

This exercise was inspired by my friend Gia Mora, a talented actor and singer who often performs on my podcast. Mora has appeared in movies and TV and created a one-woman musical comedy about science that toured around the country, but, like almost everyone who attempts this life, she did not become the next Jennifer Hudson. That's Hollywood, where talent guarantees nothing. As she's made her way into her thirties, this means she's had to try on many new identities. That led her to work as a science communicator and advocate for diversity in STEM. She even helped grow a golf accessory company. She explored activism. She composes music. And recently, she emailed me about a new job as an expert writer for one of the world's largest sustainability websites.

"Thus begins the transition from actor-singer-writer to writer-performer-producer," she wrote about the new job. "But oof! These growing pains are rough."

Without realizing it, Mora did something subtle but powerful with that multi-hyphenate self-description. She didn't just group together skill sets or swap one out for another. She *transitioned* herself into something new, by redefining the older parts of herself. It's a Bridge of Familiarity, by way of titles and hyphens.

It's helpful to map this out, because I'll soon be asking you to map yourself out in a similar way. Let's start with how Mora used to think of herself, which she defined with three words:

$$\frac{actor}{1} \quad - \quad \frac{singer}{2} \quad - \quad \frac{writer}{3}$$

Now she's adjusting to a new reality, and a new set of three hyphens. Here they are, reordered and in one case, combined:

$$\frac{writer}{3} \quad - \quad \frac{performer}{1+2} \quad - \quad \frac{producer}{4}$$

Look what she did. She brought the last word from her original description (writer) to the front of her new description, because that is the core skill she needs at her new job. Next, she took the other two words from her original description (actor, singer) and combined them into a broader term (performer). That created a blank space in her identity, which she filled with more of what she'll be learning (producer).

Seen this way, Mora didn't lose anything at all in the transition. In fact, she *gained.* She maintained a part of what she had before, but she also made way for the new.

Mora did the life equivalent of letting a professional organizer into your home. The organizer may force you to throw some things away, but they'll also show you how the things you already own can be condensed. Do you *really* need all that stuff sitting on your desk, even though you rarely look at it? Or can it go in this filing cabinet, thereby allowing you to utilize your desk space for things you use more often—while still feeling like you have all the things you once wanted to keep?

Our lives are similar: We put so much weight into the parts we're most comfortable with, which means that we see the particulars of our jobs or our days as irreplicable. To Mora, acting and singing were distinct skills that she'd developed and monetized in her twenties. They defined much of her life, which is why, when she outlined who she is, they took up two-thirds of the space. They are still important to her now—but by reframing them, she was able to repackage their role in this *new* life and make room for even more. She'd built the bridge.

This can work in infinite ways, for infinite circumstances. Transitioning to a new career, like Mora? Map out the skills you most identify with. Weighing personal changes in your life? Map out the things about your life you like the most.

Here's a blank chart for you to fill out. Like Mora, your goal is to start with three words, combine two of them, and then add a new one. Then the word in your old #3 spot can be promoted to your new #1 spot.

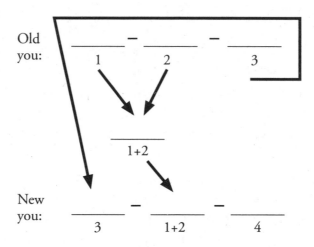

Once you've filled this chart out, you'll be able to see how, even during a period of change, you're able to give yourself *new* and *old* at the same time. In other words, you're having your cake and eating it, too.

The Theory of Theories

Sometimes a New Normal is obvious and insistent; the correct path opens in front of us. But other times, New Normal is simply a hidden opportunity in waiting. It's the better decision that you hadn't considered making, or the creeping shift that you've yet to recognize. In these cases, you can't just rely upon some external force to snap you into action. You won't just see the correct decision, even if you've already suffered through the panic and accepted that you must adapt. Now you must push yourself into action.

How? You can start by asking yourself something very important, and then committing to going wherever the answer takes you. To appreciate how to do it, I'm first going to tell you my best trick for interviewing someone else—and then I'm going to tell you the best way to turn that trick on yourself.

I interview a lot of people for podcasts and magazines, and everyone is challenging in different ways. A-list celebrities are often guarded;

they've been asked the same questions hundreds or thousands of times and have stock answers that are safe and familiar. Big-time CEOs have protective publicists, and those people have drawn up talking points for the CEO to stick to. Meanwhile, the average person is mostly untrained and unexperienced in being interviewed, which means they're nervous and prone to rambling and incoherent answers.

How can I pull something great out of all of them, regardless of their level of practice? Instead of only asking questions, I also create theories based on the things they tell me, and then I ask their reaction to my assumptions. This often jars them into a spontaneous response—and a lively discussion follows.

I often do this about halfway through an interview, after someone has gotten comfortable with me. By that point, I should have a sense of how they think and how they present themselves, and I've been listening closely to their answers. Now it's time to take something they told me and create a theory of its significance. It's as if I'm a scientist building a hypothesis, and my goal is to understand their motivation or interest in a certain area. *Is X actually the reason you do Y?* I might say. Or, *You described X as a bad experience, but might it have been useful in Y other way?* I put this directly to them, and often start by saying, "I have a theory I want to run by you . . ." They usually laugh or perk up because that isn't something they hear every day. And who doesn't love a good theory?

In 2021 I tried it on Chip Gaines, who, as I mentioned earlier, is delightful, genuine, and heartfelt—but he's also been interviewed endlessly for years, and my interview with him was booked as just another part of his book tour. Our talk started friendly, and we eventually got into the subject of imposter syndrome. He described feeling it all throughout childhood, and therefore routinely reinvented himself to fit in with different groups of kids. That feeling carried long into adulthood, he told me, and he still expects some important person to one day appear and tell him he doesn't belong in the company he's built.

When I heard that, I had . . . a theory. Here's from the transcript of our interview:

ME: I want to run a theory by you.

GAINES: Sure.

ME: And the theory, which just popped into my head as I heard you talk, is that back then, [changing identities] was not a healthy thing to do. But now I wonder if the imposter syndrome that you feel is actually pretty useful, because it's an engine that forces you to continue to build and innovate what you're doing, so that you stay ahead of whatever these imaginary people are, who are going to come tell you that you don't belong. Do you think that's true?

GAINES: Absolutely one hundred percent. And I love great dialogue like this. You're doing a great job, Jason. I'm not saying that as a smoke-blower; I mean that in a real sincere way, because it's making my brain work in a million different directions.

From there, Gaines gave a lengthy and thoughtful answer, and our interview went from friendly to truly personal. Gaines was hyperengaged. We were supposed to talk for thirty minutes, but when I tried to end the interview at our appointed time, he insisted we keep going—and we went for an hour, and then kept in touch after. But I promise I'm not (just?) sharing this because Gaines said very flattering things about me. I'm sharing it because of what else he said in his initial response: *It made him think.* That's the point of posing a good theory, and it's the reason it's such a powerful interviewing technique. It forces someone to work an idea out in the moment, right in front of you. It doesn't even matter if the theory is right or wrong; my theory with Gaines turned out to be correct, but I've had plenty of times where someone said, "That isn't quite right," and then went on to give a fascinating answer anyway.

Questions are open-ended and full of escape hatches; just watch a politician pivot away from one. But theories and observations are built on specifics. They're like mazes that people must navigate out of. They force us to confront our assumptions and to recalibrate what we know. That's why they're so powerful.

But as I said earlier, this isn't just an interview technique. This is also a powerful tool to use on ourselves—because a theory can help us step back and reassess what we do and why we do it.

Why is this important? Jon Taffer, host of the show *Bar Rescue*, once told me something that captures this nicely. "We work in our business, and we work on our business. They're two different things," he told me. "Working *in* it is the day-to-day operations. Working *on* it is when you step back, and you change things, and you grow things. Great business owners understand the difference. I have to work in it, but I better darn well save the time to work on it, too."

This can be true for every part of our lives. We spend so much time in the daily details, we forget to step back and look at the overall plan. On most days, we only ask ourselves simple questions: *How can I get this done? When is this due?* Expected questions get expected answers. If we are to recognize massive opportunities to change our businesses and lives for the better—if we are to work *on ourselves*—then we need to snap ourselves out of expected thinking. We need to see what we didn't expect to see.

That's why it's time to confront theories. Here's how.

We Can See Opportunity Everywhere, but Cannot Actually *Be* Everywhere

There are two important elements of a good theory: It must begin with something factual and undisputed, and then it must take that information and put it into an unfamiliar context.

Not every theory is valuable, of course. The world is full of people who take agreed-upon information—about wars, tragedies, and so on—and then search for someone else to blame for them. That's how we get conspiracy theories, and that's not what we're doing here. Instead, we want to build *constructive* theories that lead us into fresh and unexpected places.

Coming up with a theory out of nowhere is hard. So let's build toward it.

First, ask yourself this classic question about anything in your business or life: "Why am I doing it this way?"

If your answer at all resembles the phrase "because that's the way it's always been done," you now have an opportunity to identify a powerful moment of change. So what's your follow-up question? You might be tempted to simply ask, "Is there a better way to do it?" But that's not useful. Maybe the answer is yes, or maybe the answer is no, but neither answer reveals information. A good scientist doesn't sit around asking, "Is there something better I could do with this weird mold juice?" They instead start with a hypothesis—*What happens if I extract the penicillin from this mold, and start using it to attack bacteria?* Now they've got something to test, and a world-changing development to unleash.

Instead of simply asking ourselves "Is there a better way?" we need to spend a little time developing a theory to test. Do some research. Look at how other people and industries operate. Speak to people who are closer to the problem than you are. All of this can help you build your theory.

That's what Andy Spearing did. He's in his early thirties, and, along with his siblings and cousin, recently took over their family's business. It's called Pike Awning, and it's been making awnings in the Portland, Oregon, area since 1891—meaning it has a lot of very old processes, as well as a lot of old employees who are nearing retirement. "This is an opportunity to look at our production process as a whole and say, 'Can some types of automation or investments in tooling help fill these holes?'" he told me. That's a nice start. But it isn't yet an actual *theory.*

To develop his theories, Spearing started working all the jobs in his business—production, installing, welding frames, and so on—and asking all his employees, "Why are we doing it this way?" As expected, he got the dreaded answer: *because that's the way it's always been done.* Then he started pushing them for ideas. These employees see the waste and inefficiencies; they've surely spent a lot of time thinking about how they'd change things, if they were the boss. What would they do, he asked, if they had money to spend on making the company run better? "They've never felt comfortable to say, 'I'm going to take it on myself, to look at investments in how I can make my job easier,'" he said. But now they did. They gave him ideas—and now he had theories to test.

I experienced this myself as well, as I sought ways to improve newsstand sales of *Entrepreneur* magazine. It led me in a direction I didn't expect, and ultimately triggered a transformation far larger than I thought was possible.

It began with coverlines. In magazines, the word *coverlines* means all the headlines you see on a magazine cover. At some very large magazines, especially in the days of very large magazine budgets, publishers would test coverlines with actual focus groups. The *National Enquirer* famously built a database of celebrity magazine covers, tracking its own work along with its competitors, and broke down how individual celebrities and even individual *words* sold on newsstands. (According to *The New Yorker,* which reported on this in 2017, headlines with the words "sad last days" and "six months to live" did especially well.) But *Entrepreneur* is a much smaller company, and I don't have access to a system like that. Nor do I write about sad last days. It's kind of the opposite. So how do the cover-lines on my magazine get written?

I write them based on my own gut instinct. Then the company's president looks at them and offers feedback. Then we print it. That's it!

This process has always made me nervous. Nobody taught me how to write coverlines that drive newsstand sales. I'm not even sure that's a thing people teach. Each issue, as I work on the cover, I truly have no idea what I'm doing. That's why, one day a few years ago, I decided to put myself through a thought experiment.

"Why do I write the coverlines?" I asked myself. The answer, of course, was that that's the way it's always been done. At every magazine I've ever worked at, the editor in chief wrote the coverlines—so now it's my job, too. Then I forced myself to think about the cover differently. I am an editor, and I have an editorial background. But is the cover a piece of editorial? Not really, if we're being honest. A magazine cover is primar-ily an advertisement for the magazine—it is literally the thing that sells the magazine, and that consumers will make their purchasing decision based on. This means the words on a cover are not editorial words. They are *marketing copy*. And I am not a marketer. So shouldn't a marketer be writing the coverlines?

This line of thinking felt dangerous. In media, there's a hard line be-tween editorial and advertising (as there should be!). Advertisers of course want as much influence as possible in editorial, which is why editors have been trained to resist even the slightest whiff of business influence. I've worked at places where the editors refused to even speak with their col-leagues in advertising. Now here I was, wondering if a marketer should be writing my coverlines.

But it's an intriguing theory, isn't it? I decided it was worth testing.

I connected with a Brooklyn-based marketing and design agency called Huge. They've worked with the likes of Google and Spotify; they helped HBO launch its transformative streaming service HBO Go (which after several iterations became HBO Max). I talked through my problem with Jason Schlossberg, a managing director at Huge, and asked if I could come into the office, show someone on his team what I have planned for the next issue, and have them write the coverlines.

"Interesting," Schlossberg replied. "Let me get back to you."

He called a few days later. "Instead of just writing your coverlines," he said, "can we reinvent your entire cover?"

I wasn't prepared for this—and frankly, I was initially offended! When I first took over *Entrepreneur,* one of my top priorities was remaking the cover. With the help of a creative director, we changed the look and feel. The old covers were a mishmash of fonts and concepts, and we replaced that with clean, professional, consistent, eye-catching portraits of celebrities against bright backdrops. We felt we'd done great work. And now Huge wanted to throw that work in the garbage and start *again*? But I'd done this to myself. I asked a question, which led to a theory, which was now playing out. This is what happens when you set a change in motion: You cannot entirely control where it goes, but you can be guaranteed that it'll reveal something you hadn't seen before. I was committed to seeing this through.

A few weeks later, it was field trip time. The magazine's senior staff and I arrived at Huge's office and were ushered into a big, glass-walled conference room. There sat a multidisciplinary panel of Huge experts—people in marketing, design, copy, and data analytics. We showed them our potential cover images, what we had planned for the next issue, and answered their questions about our audience and goals. Then they sent us home, surveyed our readers, dug deep into our product, and called a few weeks later. "We have a presentation to show you," they said.

This presentation was eye-opening. It started by pointing out how similar *Entrepreneur*'s covers were to all its competitors—which was a little gut-wrenching to see. I was so proud of the new cover aesthetic I'd introduced, but now I was seeing how ordinary and uninspired it really was.

Then Huge made its pitch. Over the course of five slides, the agency told me this: "But you are different. You are *Entrepreneur*. You're a magazine for and about entrepreneurs—the very people who seek out something new, different. They don't want a regular business magazine because they don't want to be regular businesspeople. You have permission to be unlike any other magazine on the rack. Be an entrepreneur."

When I read that last line, I wanted to leap from my chair and just . . . I don't even know. Yell? Break things? I felt like I had work to do. Problems to fix! Huge was right—and what a thrill! What freedom! And yet, this also made me wonder how many other ways I was failing. How many rules was I conforming to? How many questions was I not asking? I started to feel a mixture of exhilaration and dread. This is the beauty and curse of change, I realized: We can see opportunity everywhere, but we cannot actually *be* everywhere.

Huge went on to show us sixteen cover mock-ups, which indeed were unlike anything else on a magazine rack. A few were made to look like book covers. Others aimed to make the magazine more premium or playful. Their research found that our readers love lists, so one cover simply contained a list of reasons to pick up the magazine. At the end, I pronounced myself a changed man. I wanted to do something bold and new with our covers. But that meant getting approval from our corporate leadership. I wasn't sure how they'd react.

Here I would gain yet another lesson in this process: Radical thinking builds its own momentum.

Back at the beginning of this, I asked myself a simple question about coverlines, which led to a theory, which led to me talking to Huge, and then Huge, in turn, made the devastatingly correct point about just how much opportunity I had actually overlooked. It was a snowball effect— the sense of change growing ever bigger and stronger.

I sent Huge's report to *Entrepreneur*'s president, Bill Shaw, and he found it as energizing as I did. Soon our creative director, Paul Scirecalabrisotto, was mocking up a new cover. It's a classic Swiss grid–style design with the magazine's title clean and isolated at the top, and then a framed image taking up most of the cover that we could have lots of fun with—photographing our cover subjects in an outdoor environment, or making large hand gestures, or whatever. We all loved it. We rolled out our new cover design in April 2018, and our sales have been consistently strong ever since.

After that experience, I felt changed. I realized how little I really knew about the things I'd built, and how much value can come from seeing things in a new context. I now pose theories to myself all the time, about almost everything I do. I don't think I'll ever be able to stop.

We Serve Nobody by Trying to Do Everything

When we present ourselves with an observation to test, we are challenging ourselves to rethink assumptions. The premise of a theory is that something could be better, which means that *we* could be better. When I asked myself if I should write the coverlines, for example, I was really asking whether I was the right fit for a certain part of my job.

But what happens if we go a level deeper? What happens if our theory undercuts our job entirely?

That's the theory that Kyle Hanslovan, cofounder and CEO of the cybersecurity firm Huntress, asks himself every year. He makes it a priority. On December 1 of every year, Hanslovan asks himself: *Is it the end of the line for the CEO?* "So far I've continued to hire myself, which is, I guess, a pretty good spree," Hanslovan tells me. "But I still ask myself, and plan to continue asking myself the same question."

One day, he believes, the answer really may be that he is no longer the best CEO for the job.

Why does Hanslovan do this? He says it started early. He comes from a technical background, and after forming Huntress, he thought, "Clearly there's somebody more qualified to be a CEO." But he took the job to start, because he felt qualified to launch the company and set its vision: He and his cofounders wanted Huntress to be *the* cybersecurity solution for companies with fewer than one thousand employees. (Usually, big players in the cybersecurity space focus on serving larger companies.) "When you set your goals that far ahead, for you to be able to accomplish that goal, it's going to need the best people around it," Hanslovan says. By focusing on his company's needs, rather than his own needs, his theory felt like the right thing for a CEO to do. As the leader, he should always be evaluating how his company is changing and adapting, and what it needs to create its next New Normal.

This is not just an idle exercise. It's something he does openly at his company, with a blog post that he writes at the end of every year. In it, he answers whether he's still the right fit as CEO—and then lays out what he learned over the past year that enables him to say yes, and to be the right leader for the company's next set of challenges. When it's his time to step down, he says, he'll feel no shame about it. "If somebody executed and did what they do best, why wouldn't they want to bring the next person in?" he says. "That doesn't mean you have to go. But maybe that means there's also other opportunity out there with you."

The most important thing Hanslovan said there were the words *what they do best.* Consider the implications of posing this theory to yourself. It's as if you're asking: "What if the thing I'm doing now, even if it makes me feel good, isn't actually the best use of my skills?"

Many top-level people crash into that reality, and often they are grateful for having done so. Netflix cofounder Marc Randolph is a classic case of this. He and Reed Hastings launched Netflix in 1997, and Randolph led the company as CEO. Then Netflix's growth stalled, and in 1999, Hastings suggested that Randolph step aside. "I remember sitting in the dark for quite a long time, while the office slowly shut down around me," Randolph told me. Then he went home, had a glass of wine, talked with his wife, and accepted that Hastings was right.

"It began to dawn on me that what I truly loved was the early stages—and I'll be immodest here; it's what I'm actually good at!" he says. Randolph was a startup guy. He could shape a company's vision, get it off the ground, and turn it into something special and scrappy. But he wasn't a *scale* guy—that was Hastings's skill set. So as Netflix grew, Randolph simply no longer was the right leader for the job. "The dream I had of myself as the CEO of a successful company now might have to be split into two dreams," he recalls. "I was going to have to choose which one was more important—the me-as-CEO part, or the big-successful-company part."

This wasn't a bad thing. This was actually a *good* thing! Stepping down, Randolph says, was "probably the best decision I ever made at Netflix." The experience helped him recognize his strengths, and now he could put himself to the best use—helping other companies through their launch stages. Randolph realized, as we all must, that we should identify and lean into our strengths, rather than dilute our strengths with all the things we're not good at. Think of it like this: In basketball, Shaquille O'Neal transformed teams and helped win championships because he was so strong near the basket—so who cares if he couldn't shoot a three-pointer? Nobody expected him to, and he'd have been a far worse player if he always tried both. The same is true for every part of our lives: We are good at some things, and bad at others, and we serve nobody by trying to do everything.

Randolph didn't realize this until the moment confronted him. Hanslovan is preparing himself—which is something we can all do right now, by posing the right theories to ourselves. We should challenge ourselves even if a theory is hard to hear. In fact, we should do it *especially* if a theory is hard to hear. Because the result, whatever it is, may unlock something we'll one day be grateful for.

chapter 12

What Is This For?

Here is a story that drives me absolutely crazy—but that can also tell us a lot about how we misunderstand our New Normal.

About a decade ago, the comedian Aziz Ansari met with Massachusetts Institute of Technology professor Sherry Turkle to discuss, in Turkle's words, "our mutual interest in the psychology of texting." Here's how she described the experience in 2013 (years before Ansari's popularity was bruised during the #MeToo movement), in an essay she wrote for *The New York Times:*

> As we walked through Los Angeles, people approached him every few minutes not to ask for an autograph, but to demand a photograph.

Wait, let's pause to appreciate the bias and assumptions in her language. She begins with a neutral verb: People might "ask" for the autograph, which she sees as the more natural thing to want. But today, she observes, nobody wants a scribble on paper. She uses a very different verb to describe the more modern desire: People "demand" the photo. OK, onward with the paragraph . . .

> Mr. Ansari is gracious to his fans. He explained that instead of a photograph, he would offer a conversation. He inquired about their taste in music, what they liked about his performances, his stand-up, his sitcom *Parks and Recreation*. His fans were mollified but they were rarely happy. They had to walk away with nothing on their phones.

Turkle presents this as a symptom of a larger cultural problem. Ansari wanted to *connect,* but his fans didn't want that at all. In fact, they seemed incapable of it. If you're at all familiar with Turkle's work, which includes seven books, a TED Talk (title: "Connected, but alone?"), and an endless trail of media coverage, then you'll know this is a classic moment for her. She is constantly drawing terrifying ideas out of otherwise ordinary uses of new technology, to build an argument that modern technology is destroying "the most human thing we do," which is to connect and communicate with one another. "Technology doesn't just do things for us," she wrote in that *Times* essay. "It does things to us, changing not just what we do but who we are."

In our four-phase journey through change, I'd say Turkle is perpetually stuck at Panic. She's following the same pattern as John Philip Sousa when he believed that phonographs would destroy lullabies and engineer a generation of machine babies: They both identify a moment of change, equate it with loss, and then extrapolate outward in the belief that something new will wholesale replace something old. In this telling, Ansari's fans are not just selfish and damaged for wanting (no, demanding!) a selfie with this celebrity; they are victims of what Turkle's essay called "the documented life," where we prefer *documentation* over actual *living*.

This is a tidy example of our broader cultural anxiety about change, and how, as we confront a New Normal, we often miss opportunities by seeing them through an old lens.

As we've discussed earlier in the book, when change comes for us, we tend to see loss before we see gain. And every little thing, like an Ansari fan being disappointed to talk with him, seems like evidence of this corruption.

But I have a four-word question that unravels it all.

As we are grappling with our New Normal, this question can help us find a way forward rather than send us back to Panic. It also helps us recognize the resiliency of old things, and appreciate the untold usefulness of new things. If we're feeling lost at sea, this question is like the compass that must be regularly checked. It is a question with a shocking amount of power.

That's a lot of buildup, I know. And I did it because the payoff is going to sound so wimpy . . . until you truly understand it.

Here is my powerful, simple, four-word question: **What is this for?**

If you think you know the answer, ask again. You may be wrong—and the answer makes all the difference. Let's dig into it more, and then come back to look at Turkle's situation (and every change you may be experiencing!) in a very different way.

What. Is. This. For?

I know—it sounds obvious, as if I'm asking what a can opener is for. (It's for opening cans!) But when we're experiencing change, this question is paramount. If we don't push ourselves to ask and answer this question, we'll be stuck doing the same old thing even as the world passes us by.

That's because old things can come to serve new purposes, and new things can serve old purposes. If we never challenge our assumptions about what something is *for,* then we cannot put our current experiences into proper context.

Here's a fun example from history. In the 1930s, people needed to clean their walls a lot. Homes were heated by coal-based furnaces, which covered their wallpaper in soot, and so there was a large market for wallpaper cleaners. A soap company called Kutol Products discovered that by combining flour, water, salt, borax, and mineral oil, they'd create a clay-like substance that could be rolled along walls to collect the soot. The product was popular until the 1950s, when the market shifted. People started heating their homes with oil, gas, and electricity, which meant no soot on the walls, which meant no need for Kutol Products' clay. Does Kutol give up? It does not. It asks the magic question: *What is this for?* Their product used to be for cleaning wallpaper. Now maybe it's for something else. A nursery school teacher named Kay Zufall brought the stuff into her class, where the children loved playing with it, and then she told her brother-in-law about the experiment—because her brother-in-law, Joseph McVicker, was a principal at Kutol. It turns out the clay is a great toy—and because it's nontoxic, it's safe for kids. Now Kutol has an answer to its question. *What is this clay for? It's for fun!* The company reformulated the product and gave it a new name: Play-Doh. A classic was born.

Consider the power of that shift. Kutol saw a changing world, and then changed right alongside it. Many lesser companies would have done the inverse: They would have looked at a changing world, and then *tried to stop the change.* That's what the Eastman Kodak Company did when a young staffer invented the first digital camera. Rather than recognizing it as a part of the dawn of a digital age, Kodak didn't market the camera for eighteen years . . . while other companies had the same idea, capitalized on it, and ultimately destroyed Kodak's business.

When you ask "What is it for?" you liberate yourself from narrow thinking. You accept that there is more than one answer, and that the answer may change. You acclimate to a New Normal by seeing things as they *are* instead of how they *were*.

This question can even help guide you through crisis. For example, I recently spoke with Lena Fleminger, owner of Lena's Wigs, a Baltimore-based wig shop for women with hair loss. Fleminger once operated her shop like a normal storefront. She was open all the time and people would walk in, be greeted by her store clerk, and then browse the merchandise. But when the pandemic began, she shifted to a one-on-one appointment-only model, offering virtual consults as well as in-person appointments. This change terrified her. She worried it would add too much hassle. Would anyone really make an appointment just to buy a wig?

The answer was yes. In fact, her profits soared! Why? For two reasons.

First, the change forced her to focus on her real customers. Before the pandemic, her store was often full of casual browsers, and so Fleminger had to pay an assistant to work during all business hours. That didn't really make sense, because the people walking in off the street were not serious customers. "Wig shopping is highly personal and often sensitive," Fleminger told me. Her real customers turned out to prefer a private shopping experience, and that means the people who make appointments are a self-selecting group of serious buyers—resulting in fewer hours in the office and a 22% rise in profits.

Second, the change highlighted an underutilized asset: the Lena's Wigs website. Pre-pandemic, Fleminger focused very little on her online store because she believed that a website couldn't offer the same personal touch as an in-store meeting. But during virtual consultations, as she connected with her customers wherever they are, she discovered that she could essentially bring her store to *them*. Her site's conversion rate soared; so far, nearly 100% of her virtual appointments buy a wig, and 80% keep their online purchases.

As a result of this, Fleminger's business model has changed. And here's a delightful irony: "Business has gotten so busy with my new appointment-only system that I've had to hire an assistant again," she said. But this time, her assistant is working more efficiently and for fewer hours, and Fleminger's business is growing faster than it ever had. "The pivoting forced me to reevaluate and streamline and that's been hugely valuable."

Now consider what happened there. Lena's Wigs was already successful, and Fleminger always wanted to make it more successful, but appointment-only operations and virtual consults never occurred to her before. That's because she'd defined herself narrowly. She was asking herself, *How do I do a better job of operating this storefront?* Framed that way, she'd created a boundary without realizing it. But the pandemic forced her to ask a very basic question: *What is this storefront for?*

The new answer: *It's a space to solve someone's very intimate problem.*

With an answer like that, the idea of closing the store's front door suddenly made sense.

This is the power of my simple little question. *What is this for?* The answer may change over time, which is why you have to keep asking it.

This kind of thinking can help us understand the business we're in, or the real value of our actions. We can ask it at the beginning of something, or in the middle of something, or at the end of something. Imagine asking it about a relationship that just ended. What was the relationship for? It clearly wasn't for marriage, but maybe it was for learning and self-discovery.

I want you to ask this question constantly about everything you do. That is why, on the next page of this book, I've printed this . . .

WHAT IS THIS FOR?

What's that page for? It's for you. Go ahead—rip it out of the book. Stick it on your desk or wall, or wherever you do most of your work. From time to time, look at it. If you feel change coming anywhere in your business or life, ask yourself this question. Really push yourself with it. You may have a certain skill, or have developed a certain kind of relationship, or are providing a certain kind of service—whatever it is, the question needs to be asked over and over again. What role does this thing play in your life, and in other people's lives? And has that role shifted? Is something now missing? Is there an opportunity lost?

There's a simple beauty here: When your answer to the question changes, you may not need to make some kind of radical shift as a result. Fleminger didn't *close* her store, for example. She just rethought what her store is *for*.

A New Purpose

You don't have to own your own company, or create your own product, in order to use this question at work. It may simply light a way forward for you, and help you understand whether you're making the right decisions and aligning yourself with the right people.

For example, here's my own personal journey with this question—and why I believe the entire media industry will be going on this journey, even if they don't know it yet. (It's also a good example of impending Panic.)

I do a lot of keynote speaking, and my big subject (surprise!) is *finding opportunity in change*. After I speak, someone inevitably asks me this question: "Jason, you still make a print magazine even though most people read online. Why? And will that change?"

That's a great question. I've thought a lot about it. Because of course, I worry for my industry. It's going through massive change, and very few media brands (or media executives) are as adaptable as they should be.

But I have an answer, and I believe in it strongly. I think that for media companies to survive, they have to ask themselves this question: *What is content for?*

The answer, I believe, will prove that media companies need to get out of the content business.

I have been hired to speak at media industry conventions, and when I say this, people literally get up and walk out of the room. That's too bad, because I think they need to hear it. If you're a media company, and you aren't asking this question, then you are going to die. To survive, you absolutely must get out of the content business. But that's not to say content is worthless! So again, let's ask the question: What is content *for?*

In the days before the internet, when there was a great hunger for print newspapers and magazines, this question had an obvious answer. From a business standpoint, content was for making money. You produced content, and you sold advertisements that ran alongside the content, and you also sold subscriptions so that people would get this bundle of content and advertisements. Money on top of money.

Now the game has changed. Subscriptions are way down at almost every media outlet. Advertising is difficult and unpredictable, as big sponsor dollars continue to shift toward the likes of Google and Facebook. Content is an increasingly hard thing to monetize. So what does a media company do? Well, if you're a traditionalist, you might say, *We must convince people that they want all this content. We'll make more content, and we'll make cheaper content, and we'll blast it all over the internet.*

That is the recipe for a downward spiral. The content becomes cheaper, which means fewer people want it, which means it becomes even harder to monetize, which means it must become even *cheaper* to produce, which means even *fewer* people want it, and so on.

But if you ask my question—*what is the content for?*—you start to reveal an interesting new way forward. Because content does have a purpose. It's just a different one than it used to be.

Today, I believe, content is for building relationships. People trust a media outlet because of its content, even if they don't regularly read it. This is one of the many reasons that so many product brands get into content! Think about Red Bull: That is *the* go-to brand if you love extreme sports. They produce a magazine and videos and events and a robust website and all sorts of cool stuff. But does Red Bull make its *money* off this content? No. It makes its money off energy drinks. The content is for relationships.

OK, if content is for relationships, then let's ask the next logical question: What are relationships for?

The answer is, relationships are an opportunity. An opportunity to provide products and services that people will pay for, because of the trust that has been built by the content. Now you understand what I mean when I say media brands need to get out of the content business. They must stop thinking of their core product as content! Instead, they must produce great products and services that people will buy *because* of the trust built through the content. You're seeing this happen already. *Atlas Obscura,* once a website about weird things around the world, is now transforming into a travel company. *Entrepreneur,* once just a publisher of information for entrepreneurs, is now starting to offer a range of services, from online courses to coaching people through how to franchise their business.

An entire industry was disrupted, but it wasn't destroyed. The business model shifted, but it doesn't mean that everything these businesses were doing has to be thrown in the garbage. Content still matters, but it now matters in a different way. That's why we need to ask, "What is this for?" The answer doesn't destroy our foundation; it just gives us a new purpose.

What the Overlooked Stuff Is For

The question "What is it for?" does not only apply to big, structural things about work. It can help you think deeper about every part of your life, including small things whose functions seem perfectly obvious. Maybe there's a better way to use them.

Here are three examples—about the way we talk to others, talk about ourselves, and spend our time.

1. What is small talk for?

Small talk is the world's easiest punching bag, because it has no obvious defenders. Nobody wakes up in the morning thrilled to discuss the weather with total strangers. But what if small talk is actually for something? "The reason why people hate small talk is because they don't understand what it is," my friend Joe Keohane told me. "It's not a conversation. It's a window to a better conversation."

Keohane is not a small-talk kind of guy. We have complained regularly to each other about how much we despise idly discussing our children's habits with neighborhood parents. It is boring. It is tedious. But then Keohane wrote a book called *The Power of Strangers*, which explored the importance of connecting with others, and that sent him off interviewing experts in the field. One of them was a social anthropologist named Kate Fox, who wondered why the British talk about the weather so often. So she studied these conversations and where they led. "What she found was that small talk isn't the intended end," Keohane said. "Small talk is a way to establish mutually that you're both people who are capable of interacting."

Human interaction is governed by filters. We want to ensure that the people we engage with are safe, coherent, and possible to connect with—that we're all seeing and experiencing a version of the same thing. It's one of the reasons we love commonalities; studies have found that we are more invested in other people whom we have things in common with, even if those things are meaningless, like sharing the same birthday. Small talk, therefore, is not the result of lacking an imagination. It is a well-honed filter, developed across the evolution of culture, to solve the problem of encountering many strangers who we have little time to evaluate, by helping us find commonalities. Small talk gives us an easy way in; it's a method to search for more meaningful shared interests, and hopefully build a more purposeful connection. That's what it is *for*.

Once you know this, you can think differently about your own interactions—just as Keohane did. Before his research, he had stopped chitchatting with strangers; he had shrunk more into himself. But afterward, he felt emboldened to speak with anyone, and create the opportunity for new and meaningful relationships. After all, now he knows that small talk isn't a burden or a waste of time. It is *for* something.

And while we're on the subject of talking with others . . .

2. What is an introduction for?

That's simple, you might think: An introduction is for orientation. When you introduce yourself to another person, you are explaining who you are and what you do.

I used to think that way, too, until I met a high-ticket sales coach named Myron Golden. He tells people that when they introduce themselves in any kind of business setting, their goal should *not* be to explain who they are and what they do. Instead, they should explain what they can do *for someone else*. An introduction isn't for orientation, Myron believes. It is a means for communicating value—which also means that it's an exercise in clarifying your value.

I first met Golden in an online audio chat room, where people were asking him questions about growing their business. One woman introduced herself as a "transformational coach," and as soon as she said those words, Golden stopped her. "What does that mean?" he asked. She said she helps people transform their lives. "Transform them how?" he asked. She gave an equally vague answer. Then Golden laid out a master class in how self-description is the first and most powerful piece of information a person has—and how she was flubbing it.

I was so impressed that, afterward, I emailed Golden and asked to talk.

"A lot of people will say, 'I'm a doctor' or 'I'm a mechanic.' That doesn't mean anything," he told me when we connected. "People can only decide whether or not they want to do business with you based on the fact that they hear what you say, and then they think, 'I need that' or 'I don't need that.' You want to be one of those two reasons—it's like, hate me, or celebrate me. But whatever you do, don't just tolerate me because I'm confusing."

He's developed a formula for how he believes everyone should describe themselves. It has four qualities, he said: First, a self-description must be measurable—it must contain an exact, quantifiable thing. Second, it must be stateable—it should fit into a sentence, or be spoken in about seven seconds. Third, it must be understandable—delivered in third- to fifth-grade language, to avoid any confusion. And fourth, it must be desirable—it must contain something that other people already want.

As Golden spoke, I realized how little of this I do myself. I used to just tell people that I'm a magazine editor. Once I started speaking and consulting on the subject of change, I began saying, "I help people become more adaptable." That line fails most of Golden's standards: It is not measurable, it is only partially understandable (adaptable *how*?), and it is only possibly desirable (because many people probably already think they're adaptable). Golden, meanwhile, describes himself this way: "I help high-level entrepreneurs create high-ticket offers, convey high-ticket offers, and convert those high-ticket offers so they can have six- and seven-figure days."

That explanation won't be for everyone—but it will *definitely* be for someone. He wants the right people to notice him. And that, to him, is what an introduction is for.

3. What is your time for?

People often say that time is their most valuable resource. But we don't often think about what our time is for. What is the purpose of it? This doesn't have to be a philosophical or religious question, though you can certainly take it that way. Instead, it can also be a practical one.

I once met a guy who tackled this question with stunning systematism.

His name is Sonny Caberwal, and he's a serial entrepreneur with three young children. It's a busy life: He has spent a lot of his career traveling for work or immersed in projects, and this meant that he struggled to make time for much else. So a few years ago, he decided to put all 168 hours of his week on a spreadsheet, and then track how he spent each one. The tally: 30% sleep, 30% work, 25% family and friends, and the rest was what he called "learning and general maintenance."

"I realized I wasn't making the most of those hours," he told me.

For example, he was often getting home from work at 8 p.m.—in time to put his children to bed, but hardly early enough to spend quality hours with them. What would happen, he wondered, if he rearranged his schedule so that his family time happened from 3 to 8 p.m. instead? Then he decided to run an even more ambitious experiment. He front-loaded his week with work—pulling 18-hour days on Monday and 14-hour days on Tuesday, but then tapering off more significantly the rest of the week (10 hours on Wednesday, 6 on Thursday, and 4 on Friday). He tried it, liked it, and realized that he could spend his off-hours more meaningfully, too. For example, he wanted to learn to play the guitar—but if he did it with a friend, he'd now be accomplishing "learning" and "friend" time simultaneously, while making both more meaningful.

The experiment didn't last forever, but it did give him a lasting awareness of how he spends his time. And after he told me about it, I started to think of my own time differently.

I do a lot. Sometimes it's too much. I don't want to work nonstop—that only ends in burnout—but I want to make sure I'm using my time as wisely as possible. So I started measuring time in terms of outcome. I'd ask myself: *What do I get for this next hour spent? What can I show for it later?* (In effect, "What is this hour for?") Let's say it's 8 p.m., the kids are asleep, and my wife is busy. I love watching basketball—I could do that myself. Or I could scroll through Twitter, which is satisfying in a mindless way. Or I could work on the script for the next episode of my podcast.

If I'm thinking about time in terms of outcome, I'm now wondering about the result of this time spent. *A week from now, what would I rather say I did because of this hour?* Will I remember the basketball game? Will I remember the tweets I read? Or will I be proud when people listen to my next podcast episode? In this case, the choice becomes clear—I work.

But this mode of thinking doesn't *always* lead to work, because that's not the only important outcome of my time. Let's change a factor. Now it's 8 p.m. and I'm with family. My dad and brother-in-law also enjoy watching basketball, so we're going to do that. The next hour is *for* something else: It is for better family relationships. Work and Twitter would distract from that outcome.

There may never be time for everything, but I came to realize that there is always time for plenty. It's just a question of what time is *for*.

What a Selfie Is Really For

Now that we've established how familiar things can serve new purposes, let's turn back to Aziz Ansari and Sherry Turkle. To recap: The celebrity and the technology critic are walking around Los Angeles. Fans ask Ansari for a selfie. He declines, and instead tries to chitchat with them. The fans leave dissatisfied.

Turkle claims this is evidence of a damaging change: New technology has driven a wedge between individual humans, and that's why people value a photo more than a conversation.

But look what happens when we apply our question to this situation. *What is an interaction with a celebrity for?*

Ansari and Turkle have an answer to this. They believe it is for deep human connection. Let's assume that Ansari always tried to engage his fans in conversation, even when he was *not* attempting to make a point with an anti-technology academic. That would be unusually generous of him. And it would seemingly be rooted in a belief, which Turkle shares, that there is an ideal, pure, and uninterrupted way that people should connect, which dates to sometime before the changes wrought by modern technology.

But what if fans don't want this kind of interaction from Ansari—not because of selfies, but because they literally have no idea what to say to him? He is a celebrity, and his fans are used to having a transactional relationship with him: He produces things, and they consume those things. Many are likely intimidated by him. When he asks them questions, they may worry that their answers bore him. They may not want to take up much of his time. I've experienced all of this myself: I have met and taken selfies with many amazing celebrities, but often had nothing meaningful to discuss.

What does the fan want instead? Here's what I think: The fan wants the thrill of meeting a celebrity, minus the anxiety of having to interact with them. This isn't because they've lost the ability to connect with other humans. It's because they're making a conscious decision about which humans they connect with. A celebrity will not become their friend, but they would like to share the experience of meeting a celebrity with their *actual* friends—and that's a big part of why they want that selfie. Sure, they may also post the selfie on social media, but who cares? They're proud and want to show it off.

What, then, is an interaction with a celebrity *for*? Here's the answer: It is for strengthening relationships with friends, and it is *not for* strengthening a relationship with the celebrity in the photo.

If you cannot see the world as an ever-changing place full of variety, you will apply old standards to new experiences. In the service of some outdated ideal, Ansari made his fans uncomfortable and anxious. That serves absolutely nobody.

A selfie beats an autograph, and sometimes it even beats a conversation. It just does. That's what it means to recognize a New Normal. We must know what things are for.

Once we do, we can move on to the most important phase of change.

PART 4

Wouldn't Go Back

We panicked. We adapted. We found a new sense of normal. And now we're at the phase that makes it all worthwhile—when we identify something so valuable to us that we'd never want to go back to a time before we had it.

As we enter this phase, however, I want to offer a word of caution: Sometimes, our Wouldn't Go Back moment is an obvious and exciting one. But other times, it may look like the exact opposite of what we once wanted. Consider the story of the teddy bear, which I believe is America's greatest forgotten national moral crisis.

Perhaps you've heard that the teddy bear is named after US president Theodore "Teddy" Roosevelt. That's true, in a way. Back in 1902, before anyone had seen a plush toy bear, Roosevelt went on a bear-hunting trip with Mississippi governor Andrew H. Longino. Roosevelt was a big-game hunter but had poor luck on the trip. That's why one of Roosevelt's assistants ran out, corralled a black bear, tied it to a willow tree, and then brought Roosevelt over so he could shoot it. Roosevelt refused, and called the act unsportsmanlike. Soon newspapers around the country were reporting the story—the hunter president who wouldn't shoot a captured bear.

That same year, an ocean away, the Steiff family of Germany was having a disagreement. Margarete Steiff had founded a moderately successful toy company and ran it for decades, and her nephew Richard joined the company and designed a toy called "Bear 55PB"—a plush bear with movable arms and legs, which was stuffed with dense wood shavings. Steiff was skeptical that anyone would want this, but she allowed her nephew to present it at a toy fair anyway. The response was muted . . . until 1906, when an American trader bought an initial run of three thousand of them. The toy was a quick hit in America, where it became fused with the lingering story of Roosevelt and the bear. People began calling them "teddy bears."

Originally, teddy bears were thought of as toys for boys. There were two reasons for this. The first was the bears' roughness; the initial versions were dense, a little ugly, and associated with the manly hunter in the White House. But also, girls at the time weren't given toys like this. "They would have had dolls and other things that taught them adult roles," said Jennifer Helgren, a professor of history at the University of the Pacific. This meant homemaking—kitchen tools, sewing kits, and of course, dolls—because girls at the time had only one role in society. They were supposed to grow up and be mothers. Their toys therefore had to support that.

But then the teddy bear came along. It entered the home through the boys, then became adopted by the girls. To the traditionalists of the day, this was a concerning shift. In the early 1900s, women were becoming educated and entering the workforce in a way they'd never done before. Many people opposed these new roles for women and worried about the impact it would have on families. Now they saw a bear come along and replace the doll, and they entered a full-on, phase one Panic.

Here was their reasoning: Girls play with dolls because it helps them develop a maternal instinct and therefore grow up to become mothers. But if the bears replace the dolls, the girls will *not* develop a maternal instinct, which means they will *not* grow up to be mothers, and that spells doom for us all.

In 1907, this Panic found its champion, Rev. Michael G. Esper of a little church in St. Joseph, Michigan. He took to the pulpit and gave a fiery sermon. "When your little girl asked for a doll and you gave her a teddy bear, your action was fraught with a consequence that is only excusable on the ground of your ignorance," he told his congregation. The bears, he said, are "bundles of horridness, the most harmful and repulsive nature fakes ever perpetrated." They must be destroyed, he said. The future of humanity is on the line. (There was an even uglier side to this: Esper and many people like him spoke of the dangers of "race suicide"—in other words, white people shrinking their population, because of things like teddy bears, while other races continue to grow.)

Esper's words went viral, which in 1907 meant they were reprinted in newspapers across the country. Soon schools were banning teddy bears, and other priests were taking up the cause. This was a full-blown moral crisis.

Today we know a few things that Esper did not. First of all, teddy bears did not cause the fall of humanity. But if this priest had been concerned about women entering the workforce, then we can confirm that his worst fears came true. That change happened, and society and gender norms shifted as a result.

But of course, today we do not recognize this as a problem. We recognize it as progress! We do not talk about going back—we talk about how to continue the progress, and make work fully equitable. This was a fundamental, massive Wouldn't Go Back moment. People like Michael G. Esper did not want change, but the change they did not want was good.

This may be an extreme example, but it illustrates the complexity of Wouldn't Go Back moments. A moment of change may challenge our self-identity. We may have always thought of ourselves in one kind of profession, or living one kind of lifestyle, and then change comes and we end up doing or living in a completely different way. We may feel like a contradiction. We may feel humbled. We do not always get to pick our Wouldn't Go Back moment—not in a conscious way, at least. It doesn't come ordered off a menu.

But the Wouldn't Go Back moment, terrifying as it may be, can become the most reliable source of what we never knew we needed.

chapter 13

Reconsider the Impossible

In the introduction of this book, I told you about an epic Wouldn't Go Back moment—when the bubonic plague of the 1300s set in motion the labor economy as we know it. I have one more transformative moment from the bubonic plague. This one didn't just change the way we work. It changed the way we think.

Before the plague, everything felt knowable. Intellectuals of the day like Thomas Aquinas and Dante wrote guidebooks to the world; Aquinas's masterpiece was called *Summa Theologica,* or the summation of theology, which amounted to everything anyone needed to know about how to think and believe. People of the time saw a world ordered by intention: God rewarded the virtuous and punished the sinful, and your lot in life was what you deserved.

Earlier plagues even reinforced this view. Fast-moving disease was common at the time; one would blow through town every few years, claiming many victims but leaving society intact. This tended to happen in warmer weather, which is why the upper class would leave cities in the summertime (and then a certain class of supporting characters, like actors who performed for the wealthy, would follow them). As a result, the wealthy and their friends were largely spared the mini plagues—thus reinforcing that the world was understandable and predictable.

Then the bubonic plague came. "It didn't matter who you were, how good you were, how bad you were, how rich you were, how poor you were," says Andrew Rabin, whom I also quoted earlier in the book. He's the professor of English at the University of Louisville who specializes in medieval culture and law. "None of that mattered. The plague would still get you. So if you're somebody who lives in a universe that you see as basically comprehensible, this throws that all out the window. Suddenly, you're all wrong."

This had a profound impact upon the way people thought. The world was suddenly unknowable—a place with no guarantees. As a result, the next wave of intellectuals produced very different works; gone were all-knowing texts like *Summa Theologica,* and instead we got books like Geoffrey Chaucer's *Canterbury Tales,* which portrays a complex, contradictory society full of different customs, traditions, motivations, and desires. It was groundbreaking at the time. But it also represented the beginning of the way we see the world today: Life is a balance of beauty and chaos, where nothing stays the same for long.

This is a good lesson to have learned. We could use more of it today.

A knowable world is a boring world. It's one in which we have no reason to strive or explore, and where risk is not rewarded. When we feel like we know something, we stop considering what we *do not* know. Knowingness becomes laziness. We may realize this to some degree—but still, when we're given the chance, we tend to slip into the comfort of the known.

True opportunity, however, exists in the unknown.

To reach our Wouldn't Go Back moment, we must reconsider the impossible. That is to say, we take another look at the things we once discarded—the things we thought were impossible, illogical, too diffi-cult, too radical, too ridiculous to even consider—and explore whether they were the real opportunity all along.

I will tell you: Over and over, as I meet people who thrived after a time of change, they made a discovery like this. They are doing the thing they once thought was impossible. And it defined their lives.

The Boundaries We Build

Have you ever seen a dog that's been trained with an electronic collar? It is quite a thing. The dog learns where its boundary is and then never crosses it. It's as if the dog is stuck behind an invisible wall.

Now here's a horrifying idea: We humans are a lot like those dogs. We also stop short of invisible walls. We've done it our entire careers. But unlike dogs, we often make those boundaries ourselves.

What are those boundaries? They come in the form of statements. Maybe some of these will sound familiar: *I know what people want, and I know what they don't want, and I know how to deliver. I know what's pos-sible, and I know what's impossible, and I know how to stay in bounds. I know what's realistic. I know what I'm capable of. I know where the limits are.*

I often wonder where thoughts like those come from. Why did we carve up a large world of possibility and limit ourselves to just a tiny part of it? Here's my theory: When we find something we're good at, we start to define ourselves by *how good* we can be at it. But in the process, our definition of what we're good at starts to narrow.

This problem is captured in one of my all-time favorite articles, which ran in 2012 in *Harvard Business Review*. It's called "Why Big Companies Can't Innovate" and author Maxwell Wessel succinctly diagnoses this same problem we experience as individuals—but finds it at the corporate level. Wessel explores how big companies, despite their longevity and market dominance, can become so slow and clumsy. Sometimes this leads to total failure, like it did for Blockbuster or Kodak. Other times it leads to hilarious whoppers, like when, in 1974, the baby food company Gerber tried boosting revenues by releasing a product for adults called Gerber Singles. It was literally just a repackaged version of its mushy baby food, and it flopped so hard that it was pulled from all store shelves within three months.

Why can't big companies innovate? Wessel says it's simple: At the beginning, a startup is judged by its ability to identify a problem and create a solution—which is to say, innovation! But as a company grows, he writes, "organizational structures and processes emerge to guide the company towards efficient operation. Seasoned managers steer their employees from pursuing the art of discovery and towards engaging in the science of delivery. Employees are taught to seek efficiencies, leverage existing assets and distribution channels, and listen to (and appease) their best customers."

In other words, the company shifts away from *doing new things* and into *doing old things better.* Everybody in the organization starts being judged by how they can make the same thing faster and cheaper. This saps a team's ability to develop new ideas. Why did Gerber release the disastrous Gerber Singles, for example? Because the only thing it knew how to do was make baby food—so the only new idea it could come up with was to slap an adult label on its existing product.

That leaves a company unprepared and even unable to respond to something new—particularly because disruption often comes from the places they least expect it. Here's one example of this that I love, which was told to me by disruption expert Hamza Mudassir: Everyone thinks that digital cameras killed Kodak, but what if *Facebook* actually killed Kodak? You can make the case for it. When digital cameras first became popularized, people didn't see much value in digital photos. Sure, these digital files were convenient in some way—but they only lived on your computer, whereas people had spent decades happily putting printed photos around their homes and into albums. That's why Kodak was content with its film business. Kodak believed its competitors were *other* camera film companies, and that it could defeat them by making camera film faster, cheaper, and more efficiently. But then Facebook—a competitor Kodak never expected!—came along and became a popular, centralized, digital place to store and share photos. As a result, the masses came to appreciate digital cameras in a way they never had before. Kodak had no way to respond.

Now, why am I telling you this? How does it connect to the idea of our self-constructed boundaries, and the power of "reconsidering the impossible"? Simple. Because these aren't fundamentally *business* problems. They're *knowing* problems. This book has already explored classic knowledge failures like Kodak, Blockbuster, and Gerber, but we can find this problem at the root of more recent flops and revelations, too. Remember Quibi, which was supposed to revolutionize entertainment? The company was founded by a veteran Hollywood executive and a veteran tech CEO, and was premised on combining the best of Netflix (quality TV) with TikTok (fast and mobile-first video) into a platform that created very short TV episodes that could only be watched on a phone. It raised nearly $1.75 billion, recruited tons of A-list celebrities, and then . . . launched in April 2020, failed to find an audience, and was out of business by December. The founders said they were victims of bad timing, given the pandemic. But industry observers told a different story: They said Quibi's founders didn't understand their phone-loving audience, or why Netflix and TikTok actually work. "What was intended as a mobile-only video platform remembered the video part but forgot that it needed to exist *on a phone*," wrote a critic at *Vulture* who argued that videos work on phones when they have social and sharing components—of which Quibi had neither. And because Quibi's founders were totally convinced that their videos belonged on mobile, there was no way for people to watch them on a TV. In short, the company collapsed for a simple but profound reason: When we trap ourselves inside what we know, we stop looking at what we *don't* know.

What does the opposite of that look like?

A few years ago, Aziz Hashim was struggling to solve a giant problem. He's the founder of NRD Capital, a private equity firm that buys and operates restaurant chains—including Ruby Tuesday and Fuzzy's Taco Shop, totaling more than seven hundred individual restaurant locations. The food industry is difficult, and it's made harder by a simple shortcoming: Restaurants tend to operate under capacity by 15 to 20%. That is to say, on average, any restaurant's kitchen is able to produce 15 to 20% more food than its customers are ordering. "If you know anything about the retail business, it's all at the margin," Hashim told me. "If you fill up that last fifteen or twenty percent, you make a lot of money. All your fixed costs are covered already."

But of course, filling up that last gap is hard. Restaurants typically drive new sales by running discounts or creating innovative new dishes that people want to try. But those are imperfect solutions. Discounts are hard to afford, especially as costs of food and labor keep going up. Meanwhile, new dishes require big up-front investments—and don't always pay off.

Hashim wanted to try something different, but what was it? He knew how to own and operate restaurants, and he had already explored every solution he knew. He tried to think of something totally crazy—something that would challenge everything he knows about running a restaurant.

Normally, a food brand invests millions of dollars to build a restaurant and staff its kitchen. Then, of course, it sells its food to people. But Hashim thought, what if the restaurant didn't just prepare and sell its own food? What if it also sold *other* brands' food? What would that look like?

To find out, starting in 2018, Hashim began developing something he called Franklin Junction. He likes to think of it as a Match and Airbnb for restaurants, and it works like this: Franklin Junction identifies a brand that would like to sell its food in a part of the country where it has no restaurants, and then identifies restaurants that are in that part of the country and want more sales. For example, what if the Canadian seafood brand The Captain's Boil wants to try selling in Florida? Captain's Boil currently has no restaurants in Florida—but there are Ruby Tuesday locations in Florida that have plenty of excess kitchen capacity. This means that, with a little training and shipping of food, the Captain's Boil food could be made in a Ruby Tuesday kitchen. Then it could be sold on places like Seamless and Grubhub, where customers will never know or care where the food was actually made.

In the restaurant industry, this counts as a crazy idea. It's beyond the boundaries. It's basically like saying: *There's no point in opening an actual restaurant in a location, because you could just sell your food out of someone else's restaurant.* That's why, at first, Hashim only planned to use Franklin Junction with his own brands. He launched it in early 2020—and then, of course, Covid-19 sent the entire restaurant industry into freefall. Owners were desperate for any source of revenue, so Hashim began making Franklin Junction available to any restaurant brand. The response was overwhelming, as brands like Nathan's Famous started banging down the door. "We just can't keep up," Hashim told me back in May 2020, as the pandemic raged.

"Do you think restaurant owners are more open to this change because of Covid-19?" I asked him.

"Significantly," he said. Before the pandemic, most restaurateurs likely wouldn't have considered something as radical as this. But times changed. The industry became willing to go beyond what they thought they knew. And as a result, Hashim and all of his new partners found a novel, valuable way of running a business.

That's the power of reconsidering the impossible.

And I should stress: Our self-imposed limits are not purely professional problems. They're personal ones, too. Just imagine all the personal woes we've endured because we trapped ourselves inside what we know, rather than seeking what we don't know. This is why we stay in unfulfilling relationships. It's why we live in places that don't excite us, or complain about being uninspired even as we try no new and inspiring activities. It's why we always wanted to learn the guitar but never actually learned the guitar. It is why—speaking personally—I was bummed when some close guy friends moved away, and was telling my wife about how I needed to make some new friends, and then a guy who lives nearby sent out an email to me and a bunch of guys I don't know and suggested a "dads' happy hour," and I rolled my eyes and told my wife, "Ugh, a bunch of dads—I bet they'll talk about their kids all night." And then my wife said I should grow up, because I am a dad, and many of my friends are dads, and we don't sit around talking about our kids all night, and I should put myself out there and meet some new friends, exactly as I said I wanted to do. And she was right. So I went. And it was fun. We barely talked about kids.

The greatest ideas aren't always revolutionary ones. Sometimes they're just the things we placed outside our boundaries. So how do you get outside yourself, and take advantage of this unexplored bounty? Let's take a close look at what you know, what you don't know, and what you should know.

Knowing the Unknowns

If you want to step beyond your boundaries, it's helpful to assess what you know . . . and what you just *think* you know. One of the greatest pieces of advice on this subject came from an extremely unlikely source: It was Donald Rumsfeld, who served as United States secretary of defense.

Back in 2002, as anyone who followed the news at that time will remember, the George W. Bush administration was making the case for invading Iraq. It claimed that Iraq had developed weapons of mass destruction, but the evidence for that was questionable. In February of that year, a reporter asked Rumsfeld about the lack of evidence, and he replied by saying this:

> Reports that say that something hasn't happened are always interesting to me, because as we know, there are known knowns; there are things we know we know. We also know there are known unknowns; that is to say we know there are some things we do not know. But there are also unknown unknowns—the ones we don't know we don't know. And if one looks throughout the history of our country and other free countries, it is the latter category that tends to be the difficult ones.

This quote quickly became famous, fodder for many jokes, and even the title of a documentary about the war (*The Unknown Known,* by Errol Morris). Why? Because it sounded like gibberish. Known knowns, known unknowns, and unknown unknowns? What was he talking about! But in fact, this was not some off-the-cuff Rumsfeldian philosophizing. It was standard thinking inside the national security and intelligence world, where analysts often use something called the Johari window to take stock of situations.

The Johari window was created by two psychologists in 1955 and has since become popular in the self-help world, corporate team-building exercises, and more. In brief, the Johari window asks participants to evaluate themselves in four ways:

1. What's the part of us that we see, and that others see?	2. What's the part of us that others see, but we're ignorant of?
3. What's the part of us that we intentionally hide from others?	4. What's the part of us that we're not aware of—and neither is anyone else?

You can see why the self-help world loves this exercise: It forces you to deeply consider what we're showing, what we're hiding, and what we're unaware of. You can also see why Rumsfeld and the intelligence community find it useful: It helps organize information based on what we know, what we don't know, and what we can't know.

With a little tweak, however, the Johari window can also help us reconsider the impossible in our businesses and lives. Because it helps us focus in on what, in this case, is the most important question of all: *What do we think we know, but that we do not?*

To start, let's return to the first of those four Johari questions above, but we'll modify it slightly to ask this: "What's something we know, and that others know, too?"

There are many answers to this. You might say, "I have a low-paying job." You know it, and other people do, too. You own a restaurant, so you say, "Restaurants operate fifteen to twenty percent under capacity, and solving that problem is a massive opportunity." That's common knowledge, as we've just established. If you worked at Kodak in the 1990s, you might have said, "People love taking photos using camera film and then printing them out."

But . . . wait a second. Are you sure that you're right about that last one? What happens if we challenge our beliefs, by asking where our blind spots are? That's how we're going to modify the second question from the Johari window. We'll now ask: "What is something that other people know, but that I do not?"

We're now looking to see if our facts are actually just assumptions. *Do people really love using camera film and then printing out photos?* They certainly *did* at some point, but the past does not always dictate the present. Had Kodak looked at what *other* people knew that they did not know, they would have learned that other people were seeing the rise of social media, and how digital photo sharing was one of the most popular features on pre-Facebook platforms like Friendster and Myspace, and how download speeds were only going to increase and make photo sharing easier. Maybe Kodak should have wondered about this unknown world. Maybe Kodak's entire business had shifted from being a Rumsfeldian "known known" into a "known unknown."

Now consider how this exercise would play out with Hashim of Franklin Junction. What did he know that everyone else knew? He knew that restaurants were hard to operate, that success is in the margins, and that discounting food and developing new menu items are not guarantees for success. But what did other people know that he did not? They knew that the concept of a restaurant was already becoming flexible.

The case was clear: Food delivery is on the rise, which means consumers are increasingly not visiting actual restaurants, which means they pay no attention to where their food is prepared. As a result, ghost kitchens have become popular; you may have ordered from one without even realizing it. (For example, if you order delivery from Arby's, the food may not be made in an Arby's restaurant where people can sit down. It may be made in an industrial kitchen operated by Arby's for the sole purpose of making meals that are delivered—aka a ghost kitchen—because that's much cheaper than operating a full-scale restaurant.) Meanwhile, some restaurants have also been successfully experimenting with operating multiple brands under the same roof. The burger-and-dog franchise Dog Haus, for example, launched six new brands in 2020—all of which sell versions of the same food Dog Haus makes, and all of which is prepared inside Dog Haus restaurants. So why create the new brands? Because this makes distinct food items easier to find on sites like Seamless. Dog Haus could make a breakfast burrito, for example, but few people are looking to Dog Haus for breakfast. So Dog Haus created a brand called Bad-Ass Breakfast Burritos, which is far easier for people to find if they're in the mood for a badass breakfast burrito.

In short, other people knew that the concept of a restaurant was becoming flexible. Once Hashim realized this, too, he was able to create something that other people hadn't thought of—but that he was reasonably certain would be useful.

Try this exercise for yourself:

1. **What do I know about my situation?** For your business or career, list off the basics of why you are successful and where the limits of that success are. If you're grappling with a relationship or big life change, list off what you think is true and important about these things. Then ask . . .

2. **What do other people know that I don't?** Ask for advice from people who have been through similar situations. But also, ask yourself honestly: *Would other experienced people agree with my beliefs?*

3. **How can I illuminate an unknown?** If you believe that something is true, and then discover that you're wrong, you have just created an opportunity for yourself. Now you can act upon this new knowledge.

Soon enough, you will be forced to reconsider the impossible—which is to say, you'll reconsider the ideas that you'd discarded, or never even considered. New solutions will suddenly become within reach. Why? Because they were never impossible to begin with. We'd simply placed them beyond our boundaries. Importantly, this can even include ideas that you *have* tried, but that failed in the past. "Times change.

Customer experiences change. Customer expectations change," Go-Daddy CEO Aman Bhutani told me. It's why, when he took the job in 2019, he pushed the company to revisit past failures. "We have so many cases where tenured folks said, 'This will not work. We've tried it before.' And new people came in like me and said, 'Well, let's just try it again. What's the harm?' "

The Lurking Danger of What We Don't Know

In the exercise I just shared, you're supposed to ask yourself three questions: What do you know, what do other people know that you don't, and how can you illuminate the unknown? But before we move on, we should spend an extra moment on that middle question—because it is perhaps the most easily overlooked. After all, one of the great unknowns is simply *what other people know.*

To appreciate the importance of other people's knowledge, let's start with a military story that Donald Rumsfeld surely would have loved.

In the 1980s, during the Cold War, the Swedish navy spotted what appeared to be a terrifying new technology: A strange shape-shifting form was moving around near their coastline, making a mysterious sound. They presumed it was a Russian vehicle, which wasn't an unreasonable assumption. A Russian submarine had, a year earlier, washed up on their shores by accident, and this left the Swedes a little jumpy. But this new vehicle, whatever it was, appeared far more advanced than anything seen before. How did it work? What could it do? The Swedish military spent tons of money and time and resources trying to figure this out—and they kept it all a secret for more than fifteen years. Which, again, had a logic to it: This was a military problem that would require a military solution, and outside knowledge of this problem could cause chaos.

Eventually, however, the Swedish military had to admit defeat. They could not figure this thing out themselves. So they brought in some scientists—that is, people who had totally different knowledge sets than they did—to analyze the sound they detected.

The scientists soon identified the culprit: The military was looking at a school of fish—herring, actually—as it swam as a group, then subdivided, and then came back together. The sounds they were making? Digestive gas. Basically, farts.

The Swedish military could have saved itself a lot of time—and saved the Swedish taxpayers a lot of money—by being more aware of what it knew, what it did not know, and what other people knew that it did not. The Swedish scientists' greatest contribution was simple but profound: They looked at a military mystery and considered the possibility that it wasn't a military problem.

When we do not seek outside perspectives, we needlessly limit ourselves.

We can avoid all kinds of confusion and loss by simply being aware of the boundaries of our knowledge. There are, of course, all the dumb news stories, and all the wasted energy we spend reading them, that could have been saved had someone just spent time asking the right questions. For example, in the lead-up to the 2021 Tokyo Olympics, news made the rounds of cardboard "anti-sex" beds supposedly designed to prevent athletes from getting too close and spreading the virus. An interview with an Olympic organizer later revealed that the beds were designed in 2019, long before Covid emerged, for the purpose of sustainability, not vibe-killing. (Afterward, they were recycled into paper products.)

There are also the personal mistakes we can avoid, and the personal growth we can achieve, by simply allowing others to push us past discomfort. Had my wife not enjoyed a few moms' happy hours, for example, she may not have had the wisdom to tell me to go drink with the dads. Now I have new friends, which leads to a stronger community, which leads to who knows what.

There are the decisions we make as communities, like the feverish way people have opposed legalized marijuana in America. Opponents claimed it would lead to a spike in crime and untold harm done to the country's youth, and generations of politicians barely stopped to question this logic. Now that millions of Americans have spent years enjoying legalized weed, we can finally see the result: "The absence of significant adverse consequences is especially striking given the sometimes-dire predictions made by legalization opponents," reports a thorough 2021 study by the Cato Institute. As it turns out, marijuana legalization had "generally minor effects" on crime, traffic accidents, public health, and a whole range of other things people debated about. But it did have a large impact on state tax revenues and the creation of new jobs. In short: America spent decades fighting about a change, it finally arrived, and everything is . . . fine.

And of course, there are even more systemic and more profound implications to being mindful of what we do not know—like the well-documented impact that gender and ethnic diversity has on companies' financial performance. Here is just one example, according to a study of 2019 data from McKinsey & Company: When a company is in the top quartile for gender diversity on its executive team, it is 25% more likely to have above-average profitability compared to companies with the least amount of diversity. For ethnic diversity, that number jumps to 36% more likely. These are the benefits of having more voices in a room—minimizing the chance that people will make decisions without considering what they do not know, or who might know the things they do not.

We are quick to spin narratives based on our lived experience. Weird shapes in the water? Must be a submarine. Doing this job for a while?

Then nobody knows it better. Hate marijuana? It'll destroy us all. But while we cannot be expected to know what we don't know, we can and should hold ourselves to a higher standard: We should consider the fact that we do not know. And that someone else may know better.

Knowing Less Is Knowing More

Earlier in this chapter, I listed some statements that form our boundaries: *I know what people want, and I know what they don't want, and I know how to deliver. I know what's possible, and I know what's impossible, and I know how to stay in bounds. I know what's realistic. I know what I'm capable of. I know where the limits are.*

Imagine running all of those through our modified version of the Johari window. *I know what people want*—but do you really? Maybe people see how you're failing to deliver, but they haven't told you. *I know what's realistic*—but do you? Maybe your greatest potential growth comes from something you thought was totally unrealistic.

Remember when, at the start of the 2007 global financial crisis, banks were declared "too big to fail"? Nothing today should ever be declared too true to be wrong. Everything is up for reconsideration. Just look at the experiments happening over how long our workweek should be. The five-day workweek feels so foundational to our lives, it might as well have been the eleventh commandment that Moses brought down from the mountain. But it's actually quite new. The earliest-known use of the word *weekend* is from a British magazine in 1879, and a New England cotton mill is generally credited as instituting the first five-day workweek in 1908. It wasn't until 1938, with America's Fair Labor Standards Act, that a forty-hour workweek became enshrined into law in this country. (After that, the law said for the first time, workers are owed overtime.) In other words, the organizing principle of our work lives—the thing that feels so established as to be unquestionable—only officially began the same year Kenny Rogers and Joyce Carol Oates were born. Now some people are finally questioning it. Microsoft Japan ran a four-day workweek experiment with its staff, and it found that productivity soared by 40% and electricity costs fell by 23%. A New Zealand trust management company called Perpetual Guardian ran a similar experiment and found a 20% boost in worker productivity and a 45% improvement in people's work-life balance. These experiments are surely just the start. There is simply no good reason that we work the schedules we do, and for that matter no good reason that we do a lot of what we do, except that we've done it for so long that few people stop to question its wisdom.

We will be forced to challenge our assumptions at some time, on issues large and small, whether we want to or not. We can do it proactively or we can wait until crisis shoves us beyond our boundaries. Either way, we will eventually discover that we do not know as much as we thought we do. Opportunities exist where we thought they did not. And once we learn this—*however* we learn this!—we should hang on to the lesson tightly and let it guide us in the future. Because the more we reconsider the impossible, the more we'll shift those statements we tell ourselves. Then we can tell a different narrative, which goes like this:

> I think I know what people want, what they don't want, and I'll do my best to deliver. I've seen what's possible, but I don't know what's impossible, which is why I'll keep pushing beyond the boundaries. I will find what's realistic. I will find what I'm capable of. Nobody ever truly knows where the limits are.

chapter 14

Get to the Second Time

The first keynote speech I ever gave was in 2015, in a conference room in Scottsdale, Arizona. I had no idea what I was doing. I had practiced for hours the night before, pacing back and forth in my hotel room, staring at the wall as if it were the audience. But I had no training. Nobody had ever heard my speech before, much less given feedback on it. I was going in blind—speaking to an audience of entrepreneurs and feeling very unqualified to do so.

I remember standing on the side of the stage, as the emcee introduced me. I remember feeling deeply uncomfortable in my suit—because even though I hate suits, I wore one because I thought the audience would take me more seriously in it. I remember looking out at the crowd, who appeared curious and expectant. I was opening up for Marcus Lemonis, the host of CNBC's *The Profit,* and I remember wondering if he'd catch any part of my talk, and what he'd think. And most important, I remember searching for something in myself—some idea or perspective that could help me through this moment and embolden me to get on that stage.

Then a sentence popped into my brain. I told myself: *I cannot wait to do this the second time.*

I instantly felt calmer. The very logic of it felt soothing. The existence of a "second time" meant that this first keynote I was about to give—whether it was a success or a failure—would not be defining. I was about to go through a necessary gauntlet, and on the other side of it was a better, more experienced version of myself.

There's that classic line from a Robert Frost poem, "The best way out is always through." How true it is. A career change had brought me to that stage, at that moment. I'd just joined *Entrepreneur* magazine, and I was now expected to give talks like that one. Nobody had asked me to do this before. I recognized, in some vague way, that there was a lot of opportunity in this: If I became good onstage, I'd become a better ambassador for *Entrepreneur,* and perhaps I'd even be able to make money as a professional speaker. But at that moment, I was trapped in my own inexperience. I was a guy trying to meet a new set of expectations, but without the tools to do so. The only way out of this situation, as Frost wrote, was through.

I cannot wait to do this the second time. I liked how that sounded. The second time represented progress. It meant I'd be better, and more equipped, and changed. It would be the beginning of my Wouldn't Go Back moment, when I became so good at public speaking that I'd never want to return to a time before I had that skill. All I needed to do . . . was go onstage and be worse than I wanted to be. Because that's how I'd learn.

And that's what happened. It wasn't dramatic: I did the talk, it went OK, I learned a lot, and then I did it again and again, refining along the way, until I became comfortable. A video director I once worked with told me that I should dress the way I'll be most relaxed, because my comfort matters a lot more than what I'm wearing, so I eventually ditched the suit for a T-shirt. Soon I was having fun and making money. I felt changed for the better. And most important, I felt armed with a solution to anytime I felt nervous about trying something new, whether it was going live on television or pitching a giant client. I'd just tell myself: *I can't wait to do this the second time.*

Along the way, I also discovered that great leaders tell themselves something very similar. But they'd add their own spin and perspective.

In 2021, we put the actor Ryan Reynolds on the cover of *Entrepreneur.* We did it because he transformed himself into a brilliant advertising executive, with his agency Maximum Effort regularly lighting up the internet with viral ads. (He has since sold the agency and now serves as its chief creative officer.) He and I spoke about his experience transitioning into an industry he knew little about, and I related deeply to his answer:

"I always say that you can't be good at something unless you're willing to be bad," he said. "And as I've gotten older, I've gotten way more comfortable with not having the answers. I think it's such a great tool of leadership being able to say, 'I don't know.' The worst leaders I've ever worked with or been around are the ones who are steadfast and indignant in their righteousness, and really worried about the image around them. So I love saying, 'I don't know.'"

This American Life creator Ira Glass goes a level deeper with his advice. In a video produced by the now-defunct cable network Current TV, he spoke about how, in the beginning of anyone's creative journey, there will be a large gap between their *tastes* and their *abilities.* Which is to say that they know what quality looks like, and they are unable to produce it themselves. "Your taste is good enough that you can tell that what you're making is a disappointment to you," he said. "A lot of people never get past this phase. They quit. Most everybody I know who does interesting, creative work went through years [of this]." The goal of any beginner, therefore, is to accept this gap—and accept what's required to close it. "It is only by going through a volume of work that you will close that gap, and your work will be as good as your ambitions."

While Glass's advice is aimed at beginners, Mindy Grossman offers a version of it for experienced leaders. She's a seasoned corporate leader who served as CEO of WW International (formerly Weight Watchers) and HSN, and we spoke about how to lead through crisis. The biggest key, she said, is simply to act and learn. "If you made a decision, and then you realize you needed to pivot, you can pivot," she said. "But not making a decision is really what is going to hold you back, rather than being decisive with the right objective."

All of this is good advice, of course, but that doesn't make it easy to execute. Sure, it's easy to *say* that I can't wait for the second time, or that I need to be OK having better taste than abilities, or that "I don't know" makes for powerful leadership. But it's a lot harder to *act* on that—to fail the first time, or to know you make crappy work, or to admit you don't know what you're doing.

This is a barrier to our Wouldn't Go Back moment. We have gotten past our Panic, we recognized the need to adapt, we've started identifying our new opportunities, and now we're standing at the precipice of something transformative—and all we need to do is be OK at being bad. But we don't like being bad. People won't put themselves at risk of failure simply because Ryan Reynolds (or Jason Feifer?) said so. They'll do it because they're mentally ready to do it. Which means this isn't just a question of *doing it*—it's a question of mental readiness.

Where does mental readiness come from? That's what I asked world-renowned brain coach Jim Kwik.

The Dominant Question

After a childhood brain injury left Kwik with a learning disability, he became a slow and frustrated student. One of his teachers called him "the boy with the broken brain." Then he grew up, devoted himself to understanding how people think and learn, improved his own abilities, and now coaches the likes of Will Smith and helps teams at Google, SpaceX, Nike, and more.

Kwik told me that, when he works with entrepreneurs, he likes challenging them by asking, "What's your dominant question?" This is the question we keep asking ourselves, over and over throughout our day. It's what drives our decisions in the moment; it's what focuses our obsessions when we're alone.

We may not know our dominant question immediately, but Kwik says it's there inside all of us. Let's discuss how to find it—and if need be, change it.

Kwik was recently going through this exercise with a friend, and they realized her dominant question was this: "How do I get people to like me?" This explained a lot about her—and was a good starting point for fixing her problems. "If somebody is obsessed with that question, you could imagine what her personality is like, right?" Kwik told me. "She's self-deprecating, her personality changes depending on who she's spending time with, people take advantage of her, she's a people pleaser."

The dominant question is a habit we're programmed to have. Our brains have a network of neurons called the reticular activating system, which determines what we focus on. Kwik describes our brains as "primarily a deletion device," because its job is to filter out information so that we're not distracted by the billions of stimuli around us. "The only things that come through that filter," he said, "are the things that are important to us, that are charged by the questions we ask. Because ask and you shall receive. You ask and it directs your focus."

That's why the dominant question is so important: It determines what information we receive, and therefore how we act.

This doesn't have to be a bad thing. When Kwik started working with the actor Will Smith, they realized that his dominant question is, "How do I make this moment magical?" That drives Smith toward constant action. It's why, when Kwik joined Smith and his family on a movie set, and it was 2 a.m. and everyone was freezing, Smith tried to liven things up. He made hot chocolate, brought everyone blankets, and cracked jokes. "I realized, he's living his dominant question," Kwik says.

But even when you have an uplifting dominant question, Kwik says it can still be improved.

First, how do you identify your dominant question? It tends to emerge when you're stressed, he says, so he advises building a system to capture your thoughts. Journaling in the morning can be helpful, for example—writing down your thoughts, worries, and aspirations for the day. Pay attention to the encouraging or discouraging things you tell yourself. Look for patterns. Write them down, too.

Next, how do you install a better dominant question (or upgrade your existing one)? "One way is through repetition," Kwik says, "and the other way is having external triggers." Kwik recommends a few useful dominant questions you could adopt: *How can I use this?* is a great one. So is *Why must I use this?* To program these into your brain, remind yourself regularly to ask these questions about the things around you. Some people put a question on their phone's lock screen, and then set a sporadic timer to remind them to look at it. Others will write it on Post-it notes and stick it on their walls.

When Kwik worked with Smith, they realized that his dominant question—"How can I make this moment magical?"—could be improved. His question assumed that a moment *wasn't* magical, and therefore required him to make it magical. But that could be shifted with just a few simple words: They changed the question to "How can I make this moment even more magical?" That way, Kwik said, "that presupposes it's already magical," and that's a pretty great way to live.

As Kwik was telling me this, I reflected upon the question I most ask myself. It is, "What am I missing?" This was trained into me as a journalist—to always be looking for more information, or for whatever someone *isn't* telling me. But the question has come to dominate my perspective, too. As I've built my brand and business, I've looked endlessly for new opportunities rather than be content with the ones I have. Whenever I write, I pause to explore what information I *hadn't* considered, and whether it's better than the material I already have. If a friend or colleague becomes difficult to reach, I don't get offended; I instead wonder what's going on in their lives that I don't know about.

I asked Kwik what he thought of my question. "I think every dominant question has benefits and drawbacks," he said. "To ask 'What am I missing?' you're going to see things other people don't see and uncover and discover things that other people don't find. But some people could ask themselves 'What am I missing?' and feel that they're missing out on something, and feel an exacerbation of FOMO."

He's right—I do feel that, too. I regularly, for example, drive my wife crazy by insisting we stay out with friends long after she'd rather go to bed. But that notwithstanding, I think this question is a net positive. When I stood on that stage in Arizona, waiting to go out and give my first keynote talk, I suspect my brain instantly began asking this question. *What am I missing?* The answer was powerful: This talk will help me be better tomorrow.

And there it was: *I cannot wait to do this the second time.*

If we want to reach our Wouldn't Go Back moment, we can't simply push ourselves forward. Pushing needs a purpose. Instead, we need to dig deeper into the foundational question we ask ourselves. We need to fix the filter we've set up for our lives. Because once we're asking a question like "What am I missing?" we're more open to challenging and complicated answers.

Winning Creates Winning

Jim Kwik's theory helps us understand our minds. But even if we follow his advice, and help refine the way we think about ourselves, that doesn't necessarily mean that we'll feel prepared for endless growth. We might push ourselves past one boundary, then get comfortable with what we've earned and never push ourselves again.

What can help create a sense of constant motion? The answer is: We're built for it.

Here's one more from the work of Angela Duckworth, who famously researches the idea of self-control and "grit." She's a former teacher who became a psychologist and then founded Character Lab, a nonprofit that focuses on developing the science behind how children thrive. She's studied self-discipline in students and found that their self-discipline scores were twice as good as IQ scores at predicting the students' academic success. This then carries on for the rest of our lives. "The capacity to govern ourselves effectively in the face of temptation has profound benefits across every major domain of life functioning," she wrote. When we're facing a difficult challenge, the temptation will be to give up, or to avoid embarrassment and hardship. But what does that get us? Nothing.

When we face a hardship once, and we overcome it, we're more likely to push through something difficult again. Intellectually, we've learned something about ourselves—that we have more capacity than perhaps we thought we did. But something may be happening biologically as well. Biologists have found that when an animal wins a fight or competition for turf, it is more likely to win its next fight, too. The animal doesn't have to be bigger or stronger; it seems that the simple act of winning creates more winning. Why? "Life for the winner is more glorious," neuroscientist John Coates writes in his book, *The Hour Between Dog and Wolf.* When the animals face off, testosterone levels rise in both, which improves things like muscle mass and reaction time—but only the winner's body stays flooded with the testosterone after the match. "Through this process an animal can be drawn into a positive-feedback loop, in which victory leads to raised testosterone levels which in turn leads to further victory."

As I write this now, I'm flashing back to an embarrassing memory that I had long (and as you'll soon learn, mercifully) forgotten. I once dated a woman for nine years—starting in college and going into my late twenties. We broke up when I moved to New York, and my instinct was to immediately hit the dating scene. I joined OkCupid and entered an unknown world; because my previous experience began when I was so young, I'd never actually been on an official "date" before. I was excited and nervous and wasted no time. A few days later, I'd arranged to meet a woman named Talia for dinner.

Talia was funny and interesting, and conversation flowed easy. Afterward, she suggested we walk around the city—and so we did, for an hour or more, until we ended up back where we'd initially met, underneath the Queensboro Bridge. Talia smiled and looked expectant, but I was so inexperienced that I didn't know what she expected. Was I supposed to hug her? Kiss her? Invite her back to my place? I made a snap decision and chose the last option—because, uh, that's what twenty-somethings do on dates, right? But she scowled. "Is that what you thought would happen tonight?" she asked.

"I don't know!" I said, now panicked, and searching for some way to explain myself. "I . . . just . . . uh . . . got out of a very long relationship."

"How long?" she demanded.

"Nine years," I said.

"When did you break up?"

"Last week."

She lit into me. *Nine years, and I'm already dating? Nine years, and I dragged her out as my first experiment? Nine years, and I'm inviting women over to my apartment?* My head was racing. I felt like a fool, as if maybe I'm not ready for dating after all, as if maybe I should have never broken up with my ex. But then, to my surprise, a sense of calm came over me. My budding relationship with Talia was clearly over, but now I welcomed it. I realized that this date, disastrous as it had become, was not wasted time at all. *I didn't know how to date,* I thought, *and now I know more than I did before.*

I apologized to her. I said it was very nice to meet her. I shook her hand goodbye. Then I walked away and vowed to never end a date that way again.

Only now, in what feels like a lifetime later, do I understand what really happened in that moment. I was going through a life transition—a massive change, which I knew would transform me. On the other side of that change was a new life with a new person, and hopefully a happiness so great that I'd never want to be single again. But to get there, I'd have to fail. Probably a lot.

So as Talia yelled at me, I had subconsciously thought: *What am I missing?*

Then, without using these exact words, I had thought: *I cannot wait to do this the second time.*

And then I knew that the dreaded first time was over, and I didn't want to wait a moment longer to move toward the next one.

chapter 15

The "99% There" Problem

You have experienced some kind of change, but you are not entirely comfortable with it. This might seem weird because you're in full-blown New Normal—you've adapted to your circumstances, maybe you're already in a new job or a once-unfamiliar setting, or maybe you're already deep into learning something that you know will be transformative. But you aren't happy or satisfied. Maybe there's still a small wellspring of Panic that's yet to be quelled.

Why?

I'll tell you my theory: It's because you're 99% there. And that last 1% hurts.

This is like hiking a mountain with a pebble in your shoe: It doesn't really matter if your legs are strong enough to conquer the incline, or if your shoes grip the earth tightly enough, because if the tiniest, most infinitesimal part of that rock formation ends up underneath your heel, it can bring you to a halt. You must stop, take off your shoe, and locate that tiny part.

Sometimes, the most impactful part of a journey is also the smallest part. So how can you locate it? And how can you make it better?

Innovate in the Margins

When Miley Cyrus twerked at the 2013 MTV Video Music Awards, moralists were aghast. "We're on a moral downward spiral," conservative radio host Laura Ingraham told her listeners at the time. "What you're hearing is the end of the culture." But in truth, had you sacrificed your ears to Ingraham that day, what you'd have really heard was the echo of a centuries-old complaint: A new dance reaches mainstream culture, and traditionalists use it as a stand-in for everything they find objectionable about their own fading relevance. It famously happened with jazz and rock and roll—but the mother of all dance scandals, and arguably the very first true dance-inspired crisis, was the waltz.

In the early 1800s, European society was absolutely scandalized by the waltz. The *Times* of London, for example, called it an "obscene display" for "prostitutes and adulteresses." The British Romantic poet Lord Byron wrote a two-thousand-word poem about how much he hated the dance. A society man named Theodore Hook—who, on a completely unrelated note, is credited as the inventor of the postcard—despised the waltz so much that he got into a duel over it with a waltz-loving military general. Hook was shot and killed. Do not go dueling with generals.

Anti-waltzers at the time talked a lot about how unhealthy the dance was, and how the human body wasn't made to endure all that spinning. A nineteenth-century doctor claimed that habitual dancing would take years off your life—calculating that the average life span for a waltzer was thirty-seven years for a man, and twenty-five years for a woman. In one way, this was nothing new: As we learned from the Sisyphean Cycle of Technology Panics, fast-moving scientists can often become roadblocks to innovation. Victorian-era doctors warned that novels might make women infertile, and in the 1800s, doctors warned of a medical condition called "bicycle face"—a permanent disfigurement caused by excess wind and sun. But intriguingly, the doctors of the late 1800s were correct about the waltz: It actually *was* bad for people's health.

The doctors were just wrong about why.

Doctors noted that after waltzing, some people fell ill. "Dancers were reported to have developed bronchitis and even pneumonia after waltzing. This led some doctors to blame the dance itself as the cause," said Mark Knowles, author of the book *The Wicked Waltz and Other Scandalous Dances,* who's on the faculty of the American Academy of Dramatic Arts. Therefore, they believed, the dance itself was the problem. Our bodies were not built to withstand that much spinning and touching.

But here's what those doctors *didn't* consider, according to Knowles: The dance happened in a ballroom with no ventilation, because buildings back then weren't designed for good air flow. Things were even worse in the winter, when windows and doors were closed. Candles or gas lights would illuminate the room, which poured noxious chemicals into the air. The floor was sometimes lined with a big piece of linen called a "crash cloth," which enabled dancers to glide more easily—but when dancers traversed them, their feet released lint from the cloth that filled the air with minute linen particles. When these were inhaled, they could cause serious problems in the lungs. And on top of all that, proper women's attire at the time called for petticoats, which could be heavy, and tightly laced corsets that made breathing difficult.

In short, the pure act of waltzing was perfectly healthy. It was 99% there. But many things *around* the waltz were insane and deadly. That 1% needed to be solved before the waltz was 100% enjoyable.

Now let's fast-forward a few centuries and look at a modern cause for safety concern: electric scooters. If you've visited a major city recently, you've surely seen these things. They're made by companies such as Lime and Bird, and the first time you come upon one, you think it's a mistake.

Here's this little device, left unaccompanied on a sidewalk, available to anyone. But that's its most compelling feature. To locate a Lime scooter, for example, just open Lime's app and it'll show you where all available scooters are on a map. When you approach one and scan its bar code, the wheels unlock. Just turn the handle and zip away, fueled by an electric-powered engine that can move more than twenty miles per hour. In New York City, for example, you'll be charged one dollar to unlock the scooter and then thirty cents per minute. When you're done, just leave it on a sidewalk. Someone else will find it soon.

The scooters started appearing in cities around 2017 and were welcomed with hostility. *The Philadelphia Inquirer* summed it up in this headline: "Electric Scooters Have Brought Chaos and Outrage in Cities Across the Country." People treated these devices as a wildly new intrusion onto city streets—which, historically speaking, they are not. The first electric scooters hit the streets around 1916, and were a largely welcome addition. That year, *The* [New York City] *Sun* said scooters have "the disposition of a bronco and the guile of an eel," which is a lastingly accurate description. But times are different. In 1916, roads were awash in people, commerce, and every newfangled machine on wheels. Today roads are almost entirely reserved for cars. Which means scooters don't feel like they belong.

Soon after the scooters were introduced in American cities in 2017, the narrative turned to safety: Scooters, many people said, were too dangerous. Cities started threatening to ban them. (This, too, has a long history. In 1880, bicycles were banned from Central Park because the park commissioners thought they were a dangerous nuisance.) There is unfortunate truth to the safety concerns about scooters: People *have* crashed and even died using them (although multiple studies have found them to be no more dangerous than other transportation modes). So in one way, people's safety concerns seem reasonable: They see people being harmed on the scooters, and conclude that the scooter is the problem.

But what if the scooter is not the problem? And what if the problem is actually quite solvable?

Lime dug into its data on accidents, seeking to understand what is happening. It looked at all rides for one calendar year, starting on March 1, 2019, which consisted of roughly 38 million scooter trips. It found that 99.985% of trips involved no safety incidents. Of the trips with incidents, 93% of them were minor scrapes or cuts that required no medical attention. This left 0.0011% of all trips that required medical attention.

Lime then dug into that group, seeking patterns. It found that less-experienced riders made up the majority of these bad accidents, and 36% of incidents occurred during a rider's first five trips. With this insight, Lime launched a course program called First Ride in cities around the world. That way, people could take their first rides in controlled environments, and therefore safely move through the window when most serious accidents occur.

Now let's step back and look at these two very different situations—the waltz and the scooter. Both brought changes to people's culture and environment, and both were first adopted by young people. Both were believed to cause bodily harm, and those concerns were validated by real people who experienced real harm. As a result, both were targeted for elimination: People of the 1800s wanted to stop the waltz entirely, and people of the late 2010s aimed to take scooters off the streets.

But after a closer examination, the waltz and the scooter are found to be statistically healthy activities. They are not inherently dangerous. Instead, the problem existed *around* the waltz and the scooter. It had to do with the environment that the waltz and scooter were experienced in— the 1% problem in 99% greatness. Those problems were solvable and would result in a broader adoption of change. The waltz would transition from a scandalous dance for kids into a classic dance for all. The scooter would go from a terrifying new obstacle to a common option for urban transportation.

These two stories helped me identify the "99% There" problem. If we want to find the real opportunity in something new and potentially scary, we cannot focus on the new thing itself. We must look in the margins around that new thing—making adjustments in the places where nobody else is looking, so that we transform something from "new and scary" into "can't live without."

And how can we do that in our own lives?

To find out, I decided to ask someone who transformed millions of small businesses and reshaped the way commerce happens. His name is Jim McKelvey, and he's the cofounder of Square.

I asked him what he thought of my theory. "It's good, perhaps great," he replied, but "it depends on if someone can use this for a competitive advantage or not."

Then he explained, with two words, how to do exactly that.

But Really

First, here's what you need to know about McKelvey. In 2009, he partnered with a friend named Jack Dorsey to introduce a tiny object called the Square Reader. It's that roughly inch-long credit card reader that plugs into a handheld device, such as an iPhone or iPad, and transforms it into a digital cash register. This sounds small and simple, but it was transformative. Many small businesses couldn't accept credit cards before this; the process was simply too cumbersome and expensive for them. But now everything from food trucks to farmers' market stands could take a card. Business has fundamentally changed because of it.

Maybe you've swiped your card through a Square Reader and thought: *That's so easy!* Competitors in the payments industry saw it and thought: *That's so easy to knock off!* Then they tried—and often failed. "People thought the secret to Square's success was building a card reader that plugged into the headset jack," McKelvey told me, "but really it was the other fourteen things in our innovation stack."

An "innovation stack" is a model that defines the different types of possible innovations within an organization, and a way of thinking about building new things. The idea is that innovations are stacked on top of one another, each working in tandem to support the other. (It's also the title of McKelvey's book, *Innovation Stack*.) A credit card reader, for example, isn't very useful without figuring out how to lower the processing fees for small businesses (which is the reason so many entrepreneurs didn't take credit cards), or without completely new and innovative relationships with credit card companies. Square addressed all that. Square's competitors did not. "As a result," McKelvey says, "most of our potential competitors headed down a dead-end path designing hardware while the real opportunity lay elsewhere."

To McKelvey, this is a fundamental lesson that goes beyond business. It's about remembering that *what you see* isn't *all there is*. Or to keep with the theme of my theory, you can't confuse the 99% for 100%. "The reasons things look easy is often ignorance," he told me. "Watching a master chef poach an egg makes it look easy. Only after you have a kitchen full of gelatinous slime will you appreciate how difficult the process truly is. I've watched entire companies get funded based on an assumption that something is easy that is actually difficult. Humans love to think they understand."

Given all that, I asked McKelvey how a person can identify something new and then truly maximize it. How can they get to 100% themselves?

"Doing one thing causes another problem, but often in a surprising way," he said. To illustrate his point he reframed the stories of the scooter and waltzing that I had also shared with him: "People assume dancing is unsafe, *but really* it's the ballrooms. People assume the scooters are unsafe, *but really* it's the riders. Look for that phrase *but really* and you will find a competitive advantage."

Rewind a little and you'll see that McKelvey used that exact phrase when describing Square. Here it is again: "People thought the secret to Square's success was building a card reader that plugged into the headset jack," he said, "*but really* it was the other fourteen things in our innovation stack."

When McKelvey meets with innovators, he loves asking them this: "Tell me something nobody else knows about your innovation stack." It's a kind of quiz. If someone has created something truly new, and understands its exact purpose in the world and how it's measurably different and better than everything else, then they will have dozens of answers to this question. "Posers spit platitudes, while real entrepreneurs know first-hand *why* things happen in non-obvious ways," McKelvey said.

His advice to anyone trying to answer that question, or to just find the value in new things: "Look for the *but reallys*," he says.

These simple words may in fact be the difference between New Normal and Wouldn't Go Back. Want to get to a place where you truly, fully appreciate something new? Make a list of *but reallys*. Write down at least three of them, at which point you'll have thought so deeply about the subject that you'll probably have many more. Challenge yourself to recognize not just what this new experience is good for, or what its potential is, but what it might be missing as well.

I may be dissatisfied with my job, *but really* I'm being pushed to better identify what I love and how to pursue it. I may need to move to a different city, *but really* I'm now able to find a place that fulfills needs I didn't have before. I may have just taken on a terrifying new project, *but really* I'm learning a skill set that will be valuable later.

Once you know your *but really*, you can foster it. You can solve the small problems, which in turn can solve the big ones.

We must innovate inside the margins of our own lives. We are 99% there. That can be a problem, or it can be an opportunity: It means there's only 1% left to go.

chapter 16

Permission to Forget

Wouldn't Go Back moments come with a strange side effect: They may prompt you to ask big, scary, existential questions. Like, *Who am I anymore?*

This is natural. After all, change means giving up a part of our identity—or at least, a part of what we *thought* was our identity. It's something we talked about at the beginning of this book, when we separated out *what we do* from *why we do it.* But it's impossible to really appreciate the depth of this shift until you reach a Wouldn't Go Back moment yourself. This is when you realize that something from your past—something you once felt passionate about, and that you maybe even thought of as core to who you were—no longer feels as relevant. It is no longer a part of your story.

It's like a massive identity crisis: *I used to want this. Now I want that. Who am I anymore?*

How can we reconcile that?

As we reach the end of this book, I want to answer that question in a way that could seem like a recipe for even more existential dread—but that I think is ultimately liberating. Here's the big takeaway: Our brain is not built to remember the past perfectly. In fact, it's quite the opposite. Our memories are flexible and at times entirely manufactured. The story we tell of ourselves is not a whole truth; it is a narrative we built to get us to where we are, and it is designed to be molded, like clay that never hardens, in order to help us get to wherever we want to go next.

That's what I learned from talking with memory researchers. We discussed this briefly in the beginning of the book, but now let's take a deeper dive into how our memory works—to see what's real, what's not, and why your past is really about your future.

A Brain Built for Change

Our memories do not work the way a video camera does. The brain does not capture most events in great detail, and it does not store them as complete experiences. Instead, it divides our memories up into lots of tiny pieces, and then stores them separately. When you're in the act of remembering something, your brain is reassembling all those pieces into a coherent whole. But not all the pieces survive.

Felipe De Brigard, a Duke University associate professor who studies how memory and imagination interact, compares it to reassembling a dinosaur's skeleton out of unearthed bones. The skeleton isn't whole; it's in a pile of little pieces, and a paleontologist must reassemble all those pieces into a coherent object. But some of the pieces are missing, which means the paleontologist must use other information to fill in the gaps. We must do this with our own memories, too— and what is the source of our additional information?

It is our imagination.

"Memory and imagination are really not entirely different faculties," De Brigard tells me. "Memory and imagination are profoundly intertwined. Many of the processes that enable us to remember the past are also processes that enable us to imagine not only possible futures, but also to imagine alternative ways in which past events could have occurred."

We imagine the missing parts of our memories, and then we experience those imagined memories as real memories.

Why would we do this? De Brigard says you must consider what memory is actually *for*. (Remember my question from earlier in the book, "What is this for?" That extends to our brain functions as well.) De Brigard says that you can find a clue in a phenomenon called *fading affect bias,* which is the scientific term for what happens to our memories over time: The negative emotion of negative memories tends to fade faster than that of positive memories, so we remember good things much better than we remember bad.

That's not to say we always completely forget bad things; we can retain lessons from bad experiences. But the bad stuff fades faster; its edges get shaved off. You can see this appear in ways large and small. There's the ex you keep gravitating toward, because you forget just how miserable you were in the relationship. But also, studies have found people who expressed a kind of nostalgia for terrible events, like Polish people thinking fondly of life under communism. More recently, in 2021, there was a wave of people expressing nostalgia for life during Covid lockdown. (On Connecticut Public Radio, *The Colin McEnroe Show* invited listeners to share what they're nostalgic for, which ran in an episode called "We're Feeling Nostalgic for Quarantine Life. It Wasn't All Bad.")

Although fading affect bias isn't always productive, De Brigard said its ultimate purpose is to be a defense mechanism: "If our memories of bad events were as negative at the time of retrieval as they were at the time of encoding, it would be a very burdensome memory to live with," he said. That's beneficial—it means that, for most of us, we aren't forced to relive sad or cringe-worthy moments. We remember the fact of them but cannot conjure the experience of them. (Extreme trauma can change this, of course. That's where therapy can be helpful.)

In other words, our memories aren't designed to be time capsules. There's no biological point to that. "Remembering is not only an issue about bringing mental representations of past events to the present," De Brigard says, "but sometimes we use memories to help us at the present, or sometimes we use imagination to help us in the present." Why do we reminisce with friends? Why do we remember the happy times in our relationships? It isn't to honor or tell the true story of the past. It's to foster those relationships in the *present,* so that they're here for us in the *future.* "We spend an enormous amount of time remembering, in part because it's good. It is helpful," De Brigard says.

Now here's where it gets really tricky—because while our actual bad memories fade, we also subconsciously take good memories and *make* them bad. "In a lot of cases, we actually recall the past as worse than it was when it comes to our own personal identity," says Anne Wilson, a professor of psychology at Wilfrid Laurier University, whose research focuses on the way we remember our past selves and how it shapes who we feel we are today.

Humans have what's called "episodic" memory—we take memories from our lives and craft a coherent narrative from them. As far as we know, no other animal does this. But of course, the story we tell of ourselves cannot be our true story. Life is complicated and stories are not. "We like to see ourselves as continually improving over time," Wilson says, so that is the story many of us remember. We think of our pasts as harder and more rigorous; we imagine our earlier selves as less satisfied. When scientists track us over time, they see that our narratives don't line up with reality. "If you compare how people actually are contemporaneously over a number of periods of time and what they recall for those periods of time, people tend to shift their past downwards," Wilson says. The improvement they see in themselves is, in fact, "remembered improvement." (This may feel in contrast to the "good ol' days" myth I wrote about earlier in the book, but that's humanity for you: We're complicated.)

When Wilson told me this, it hit me personally. Because here's the thing: In my work I tell a lot of stories about myself, and I have honed these stories very well. I have already told some of these stories to you. But I sometimes wonder how true they really are.

For example, earlier in this book, I told you about my first job, which was as a reporter at a tiny newspaper in central Massachusetts called *The Gardner News.* Quick refresh: I hated that job. It was small and frustrating, and I aspired to work at the biggest papers in the country. So after a year, I had a realization: Nobody at *The New York Times* or *The Washington Post* would ever pick up a copy of my tiny paper, read my story about the local diner, and then call me up and say, "Pack your bags, we're bringing you up to the big leagues!" I realized that, if I wanted to make a career leap, I couldn't keep working at this little paper and wait for someone to discover me. I had to go to *them.* So I did. I quit the job, I sat in my bedroom in a cheap apartment next to a graveyard, and I cold-pitched for nine months until I landed my first story at *The Washington Post.* I grew my career from there, and it taught me a lesson I've carried through to this day: *Don't wait. Go to them.*

I have told a version of that story so many times—but how true is it? Parts can be fact-checked. I did quit that job. I did freelance out of my bedroom. I did land that *Post* story. But did I have that thought—*they won't come to me so I have to go to them*? Did I ever say that back then, or even think it? Or did I just quit that job because I was miserable and it paid me $20,000 a year, and it was only *later,* when I tried to make sense of a random series of earlier events, that I crafted a story on top of it?

The answer is . . . *I honestly do not know.* I've told the story so many times that there is no other story to tell. There is no other memory in my brain to uncover.

Wilson says I shouldn't worry about this. Yes, we should strive for truth. But we must accept the limitations of our memory—and the purpose of those limitations.

When scientists monitor people's brains, they see a fascinating pattern: Brain activity is very similar between when people engage in episodic memory and when they think about the future. "It may be that part of the reason that our memory for the past is so imperfect is because it needs to be malleable," Wilson says, "because if it's malleable, then it allows us to creatively use those same building blocks and reshape them into this future that we want to be able to imagine."

The future matters. Biologically speaking, it wouldn't make sense for our brains to completely limit our future options based on our past experiences. We'd never learn anything. We'd never take a risk. We'd never engage with change, let alone embrace it. We'd never say, "I failed ten times before, but this time is going to work." We *need* this flexibility; we need to tell ourselves the stories that keep us going.

This is what makes a Wouldn't Go Back moment possible. Whether we realize it or not, we are constantly revising not just what we do, but who we are and the story we tell about ourselves. Our past is only as good as it is useful to us. We may cling to it for a while; we may mourn the passing of one experience or identity. But at our core, inside our very biology, we are built for change.

Our Natural State

There's one final thing I want you to know about memory: It's how to create good ones.

Our brains do not have an internal clock or a calendar; it's why you're bad at remembering if something happened in 2012 or 2015. Instead, says De Brigard, "memory is extraordinarily sensitive to breakings of events." De Brigard calls this *segmenting*. New things create distinct memories. Similar things blur together. This is why, when you travel, days feel longer than an average day. More unique things happened, which created more segments, which means there was more to remember.

We can use this to our advantage. Sameness is forgettable. New things are memorable. Our lives are richer and fuller when we pursue new.

"The most important thing is that you're working for a future self," De Brigard says. "I mean, let me just put it this way: What life do you prefer—one in which you can have fifty experiences per week but you won't remember any, or one in which you could have twenty-five *new* experiences and remember them all? If you're like me, I hope you're going to say, 'I want to have the ones that I can remember, because there is something supremely important to having the good experiences now but being able to remember them later.'"

Panic, Adaptation, New Normal, Wouldn't Go Back. We'll remember going through them all, though imperfectly. Memories of Panic will float away—that's fading affect bias at work. Adaptation and New Normal will blend together; the drudgery will become a soup of sameness. We may come to lionize those difficult phases, as we use and inflate them to tell an epic narrative of ourselves that may only be partially true, but that helps embolden us to test fate even more. Then we will reach Wouldn't Go Back, the most memorable of them all, which is the moment we become something new. But then again, we are always *becoming,* aren't we?

We are, at any time in our lives, the sum of what came before, and the joy of what we now are, and the thrill of what could come next. In truth, Wouldn't Go Back isn't some radical discovery. It is our most natural state. We have always been prepared for it. All we need to do is believe in ourselves. And trust ourselves. And then start building for tomorrow.

Build Your Tomorrow

You now have the tools and understanding to quiet your Panic. You have questions and exercises to speed your Adaptation. You have the transferable skills and knowledge necessary to build your New Normal. And you are primed to embrace your Wouldn't Go Back moment.

Are you ready for whatever comes next?

You still may not feel it. That's OK. Nobody feels prepared for the unknown. That's why, in these final pages, we'll review how to use this book to address changes large and small. And to start, let's put it all in perspective—with the wisest, simplest advice I've ever received.

At age twenty-eight, as I told you earlier, I was living in Boston and got a job offer in New York. It was a dream job—but taking it meant destroying a life I loved. I already had a job I thrived in, a close group of friends I'd known since college, and a girlfriend whom I lived with. She wasn't interested in moving; she wanted to stay local and could not understand how this offer in New York was better than everything I already had. "When does it stop?" she asked, by which she meant, when will I stop making sacrifices for my career?

Those words haunted me, so I called my parents for advice. I remember pacing in the streets of Boston, laying out the dilemma for them. And I told them what my girlfriend asked: *When does it stop?*

"It never stops," my parents replied.

Plain as that. It never stops. It's an irony of life: We often define ourselves by the past, but we are nothing without a future. Why work for something greater, if we'll only ever have what we currently have? If I stopped now, my parents said, I might feel satisfied today . . . but what happens tomorrow? What happens if I regret not growing more, and declined a chance to do it?

This is not an easy perspective to shift into, because our days and months are generally filled with things that do stop. We are constantly working toward definitive endpoints, so the idea of having them—of working, and then *stopping*—seems quite natural. I hadn't really considered this until many years later, after I did take that job, and did move to New York, and I interviewed Michelle Pfeiffer,* who told me about her own struggle to move from endpoints to endlessness.

Pfeiffer, of course, has had a long and celebrated career in acting. When she became a parent, she started looking closely at the ingredients in products that she was putting on her and her children's bodies—and was alarmed by how little the cosmetics and fragrance industries disclosed about the ingredients they used. She stopped using perfume, which she's always loved, and then tried to convince fine fragrance companies to become transparent about what's actually in their products

---

* A personal, self-indulgent side note: Throughout my adult life, whenever someone asks how to pronounce my last name, I've always said, "It's Feifer, like Michelle." People laugh; it's a good and useful line. But then I got to tell Michelle Pfeiffer that I say this, and she seemed genuinely delighted, which of course delighted me. We Pfeiffers/Feifers must stick together.

(and then to certify that they're safe and environmentally friendly). She called around. People were happy to talk, but always said no: That just wasn't the fragrance industry's thing. So although she had no interest in starting a company, she decided to do this work herself. It took her nearly twenty years to find partners and formulate a product, but when I first spoke with her in 2019, she'd accomplished the initial leg of the journey: The company was called Henry Rose, and it was about to launch.

Back then, Pfeiffer told me how disorienting the launch of a company was to her. She is used to making movies, where the beginning is hectic, and the work can be challenging, but you can also count down the weeks and days until it's done and gone and you never have to think about it again. Building Henry Rose would be the opposite of that: She worked for years to launch the company, and was struggling to really appreciate how *launching* was only the beginning. "I'm a little numb at this point," she told me, "and not sleeping a lot." Two years later, in 2021, we reconnected and I asked how things had gone since. "I kept waiting for it to end," she said, "and I finally realized, well, it's never going to. This is what it means to be in business."

There it was: Michelle Pfeiffer, like the rest of us, grappling with the difference between endpoints and endlessness. She and I talked about how similar this is to having children. As a new parent, waking up at 4:30 a.m. to the sound of a child screaming, I can remember wondering when I'll finally get to sleep in, and then remembering that the answer is *never*. That's a shock. Until it's not. Then we discover the beauty of endlessness: It is a state of constant experimentation, when all ideas are welcome because there's time for them all. "In some ways," Pfeiffer said two years after launching her business, "the fun is really starting now."

This is why we must build for tomorrow, and it's why you must build *your* tomorrow. The potential joy of tomorrow is what propels you and gives you purpose.

You are already well equipped to do this. Now it's just a matter of doing it.

Let's look at some examples, from small to large, to review how the advice in this book could help.

Using This Book

Build for Tomorrow moved through the four phases of change. As we reflect on how to make them useful, here's a handy way of translating them into action:

Panic $\rightarrow$ Pause when others panic

Adaptation $\rightarrow$ Change first or, better yet, before you have to

New Normal $\rightarrow$ Lead the charge to change

Wouldn't Go Back $\rightarrow$ Seize new opportunities

Now let's look at four examples of uncomfortable change, from small to large, and see how to use those four phases to your advantage.

Change #1: A Change at Work

You've been at a company for ten years and have become comfortable with the job. Now a new boss has new ideas, or your company is going through a reorg, and it means you must do your work differently. "Why fix what isn't broken?" you say bitterly.

Panic: Let's be real—you're not just bitter. You're concerned about whether you can keep up. But remember, *you come from the future.* "Your way" was frustrating and terrifying to whoever came before you.

Adaptation: You've lost something familiar. But instead of obsessing over that, assume you're going to gain something, too. The question is—*what is the gain?* Ask your boss about the problems they identified with the old system and how their new one can fix it. You may not immediately agree, but it will help you appreciate the intended benefit.

New Normal: You have an opportunity here—because all your colleagues are grappling with the same change, and those who adapt the fastest are the ones who will get ahead (and maybe even spot additional new efficiencies and opportunities your boss hadn't anticipated). How can you get there? Build a Bridge of Familiarity. Start with your old goals and outcomes, see how they're reached with this new process, and then figure out the best new ways to achieve them.

Wouldn't Go Back: Change doesn't happen through learning. It happens through doing. When you're being trained in a new system, or being taught new software, or following new processes, it won't feel natural and comfortable for a while. It's the "99% There" problem—that little gap at the end will nag at you. Through repetition, you'll find value in the new. You'll forget about the old. You're doing your job better.

Change #2: A Change of Direction

You were working in one industry, and now it's time for a change. Maybe your industry is in the middle of a disruption, leading to constant layoffs and company closures. Maybe you're bored or unhappy or unsatisfied, and just can't imagine going back to work another day. Whatever the reason, it's time to move on.

Panic: This isn't just a career change; it feels like an identity change. Who are you now, if you're no longer in the trenches with the kinds of peers you've known for years or decades? You may start to romanticize the old days—the long hours, the frustrating work. Maybe it wasn't as bad as you think?

Adaptation: Don't get caught in an identity crisis. Instead, it's time to separate "what you do" from "why you do it." Who are you, at your core? You aren't the job you just did—but you *are* the reason you excelled at the job. Are you a relationship builder? A connector? A creator?

New Normal: What do you want to do next? It's OK to not know the answer. Remember Wharton professor Katy Milkman's advice: We're often afraid to experiment, because we wrongly believe that our experiments must be permanent. That's not true. "Pull the trigger on *something*," she said. If it fails, no problem—you learned something for next time.

Wouldn't Go Back: You will be bad at whatever you try next. That's OK—everyone experiences it. (Ryan Reynolds says, "You can't be good at something unless you're willing to be bad." And it's true.) As you face new challenges for the first time, tell yourself, "I can't wait to get to the second time." The first time is for learning. The first time is for betterment. The first time is for *getting* to that second time.

Change #3: A Change at Home

Your life as you know it is about to become your "old" life. Perhaps you're breaking up with someone you've dated for a while. Perhaps the rent on your home was raised and you need to move. Perhaps you've been offered a job . . . but it requires moving to a different city. Whatever happens, this change marks the end of one phase of your life and the beginning of another.

Panic: Here comes the fading affect bias—that phenomenon where we remember good memories longer than bad ones. You will romanticize your "old" life to the point where it seems it was perfect, and you will wonder if there's something—*anything*—you can do to hold on to it.

Adaptation: Start pre-morting your next moves by asking yourself: "If I made this decision, and six months from now I'm regretting it, why might it be?" You can't avoid discomfort this way, but you *can* take a fresh look at your options, pick the risks you're most willing to manage, and uncover hidden assumptions that'll help you pursue decisions more thoughtfully.

New Normal: Assess how your past experiences can help inform your next ones. Ask this of everything: "What is it for?" If you broke up with someone, for example, what was the relationship for? Maybe it was to teach you new insights about yourself, so that your next relationship is stronger. If you're moving, what is that experience for? Maybe it's an opportunity to reassess exactly what you want, where you want it, and what you must do to afford it.

Wouldn't Go Back: It's time to reconsider the impossible—the options you once discarded because they seemed unappealing or unrealistic. You can start by asking yourself three questions: What do I know about my situation? What do other people know that I don't? How can I illuminate an unknown? Now follow the answers.

Change #4: A Change in Society

The world you knew is becoming different. Young people are doing things that seemingly make no sense, and that you suspect might be bad for their health. New technology appears to be driving great social ills.

You do not know what to do, but you feel like someone—politicians? media? anyone!?—should step in before too much is lost.

Panic: Ask yourself this question: "Am I truly witnessing something new, or am I just witnessing a new version of an old thing?" History proves that it's almost certainly the latter. That is important context: Now, rather than feeling like you're being swept up in an uncontrollable current, your Panic can be a prompt to dig deeper into what's really happening.

Adaptation: It's time to be "cognitive reflective," as Good Judgment CEO Warren Hatch says, by considering how confident you should be in the knowledge you think you have. "The value is to slow yourself down so you can get to a better outcome," he said. Instead of just doom-scrolling through hysterical stories about tech addiction, for example, you could find well-informed and level-headed articles written by addiction researchers.

New Normal: Businesses often treat failure as data, but everyday people can do it, too: When our beliefs are proven wrong, we don't need to be embarrassed; we can simply use it as an insight to help inform our fuller network of beliefs. What other Panic-driven ideas do we have, for example? And do they really hold up to scrutiny, too?

Wouldn't Go Back: When we panic, we inhibit our ability to truly understand a problem—or to create a meaningful solution. But now you're able to look at things more clearly. Perhaps this means you simply save your energy; you're no longer doom-scrolling the internet, which clears your mind to focus on more important things. Or maybe you advocate for better solutions for yourself, your family, or your community. If your child spends a lot of time playing video games, for example, and you know the problem isn't an abstract "addiction," you can now dig into what's happening in their life and help them build better habits.

As you just saw, in each example I gave, I did not expect you to utilize everything in this book. That's because the book isn't meant to be a puzzle, where every piece is necessary to see the big picture. The book is more like a utility belt, full of tools that can be useful individually or in combination, depending on the situation. My goal is to convince you that they're useful—and then empower you to use them where needed.

Everything Is the Next Thing

Early in this book, I mentioned that I'd temporarily relocated from Brooklyn to Boulder, Colorado, during the pandemic. That became a more profound change than I expected.

My wife, Jen, and I moved there because, as lockdowns began, we were living in a small apartment with our two young boys, and my parents urged us to come stay with them. They have a house with more room for kids to run around, and we went thinking it would be nice for a few months. When we arrived, we thought of ourselves as displaced New Yorkers. We both love the city's aggressive energy, and, I admit, we're both a little work-obsessed. My life in New York was a marathon; I was rarely making time for fitness or mental breaks. Meanwhile, the people we first met in Boulder kept talking about weed and hiking trails. Work rarely came up in conversation. I told my wife, "Our people aren't here."

But because the school situation was better in Boulder than in New York, we stayed for eighteen months. And at some point during that time, an unexpected thing happened: I started to really like it there.

Cars? Houses? A backyard? None of this had mattered to me before—but now I watched my older son learn to ride a bike in the neighborhood, and I started to hike and bike myself, and Jen and I discovered that some of "our people" *were* in Boulder, and we made great friends. Meanwhile, my career was on fire: I landed some big deals and expanded my audience, despite working fewer hours and not being in a midtown

Manhattan office. By the time we were ready to go back to New York, I felt shaken: If I had long identified as a New Yorker, but I was happy and successful in this very different environment, then who exactly was I? And where did I belong? Something had changed—but what was it? What would be my Wouldn't Go Back moment?

Jen had no interest in moving to Boulder, so there was no point in talking about staying. On the question of New York, we actually *would go back.* But when the time came to leave, she thought it would be too abrupt to just fly back home—to depart one life, and simply arrive in another one. She instead came up with a three-week road trip, where we'd see friends and family along our way back east. This turned out to be a brilliant decision. Instead of going through one abrupt change, from our new life back to our old one, we experienced a buffet of lifestyles: We got to imagine living in different cities, saw old friends (and their new houses), and generally embraced our placelessness.

Then we finally drove into Brooklyn. As we did, I turned to Jen and said, "I feel like New York is just another stop on the trip." Arriving felt like walking into an interactive memory—as if it's a thing from my mind that other people also inhabit.

Throughout our time in Boulder, I kept joking to Jen that one day, we'd get into bed in Brooklyn and I'd say, "Well, that's over." As if we'd just gone out to dinner. As if we'd picked the kids up at school. We left and came back. Time collapses upon itself. So on that first night, as we actually got into bed in Brooklyn, I smiled and said, "Well . . ."

She laughed, knowing what's coming.

"That's over!" I said.

"It's so not over," she said.

She was right, in a way we could not quite anticipate. Something had changed. We didn't know what. And we might not know for a very long time. And this got me reflecting on the many different ways that Wouldn't Go Back can look. Because yes, here we were in the same bed, in the same apartment, in the same city as before. We came back. But what if Wouldn't Go Back isn't always about something so literal? What if we are in the same place, but we are not returning to the same exact life?

This would turn out to be true. In our old life, we didn't have a car. Now we do, and we load the kids into it many weekends and leave the city on adventures. In our old life, I took no time for exercise. Now I regularly leave my computer in the middle of the afternoon, hop on a bicycle, and circle nearby Prospect Park. I have started regularly blocking a day off on my calendar, where I will schedule absolutely no calls or meetings, so that I am not a slave to the clock and can think more ambitiously. Jen and I have talked about the possibility of moving to other cities, which we would have never considered before, or at least moving out of the trendy neighborhood we love so that we can afford more space for the kids.

We now live with options we hadn't considered before, and a balance I didn't know was missing. We came back in a physical sense, yes, but we brought along plenty of new things, too, along with a realization that more change would always come. Wouldn't Go Back does not mean hitting a hard reset on life; sometimes it just means updating the foundation.

In the past, I would have liked a greater sense of permanence: *I am here. I do this.* I think we all probably want that; it's more comfortable that way. But there's something exciting and more truthful about seeing things as part of a continuum, which they are. We don't get to hit pause—and we shouldn't want to, anyway.

A major real estate developer once told me, "If a city isn't growing, it's dying." I think that's true of people too. Growth inspires us. The possibility of growth motivates us. We wake up today in order to provide for ourselves tomorrow. We are all builders at heart.

So it may benefit us all—as it has for me—to more intentionally see everything we do as simply the next thing, but never the permanent thing. It should liberate us from the fear that every decision defines us, or that every failure follows us. Everything is just the next thing, in a long line of next things, and we should want as many nexts as possible.

Because who wants permanence in a world of potential?

Given all that, now that I look back on it, here is how I used the phases of change to my own advantage:

Panic: As I became more comfortable in Boulder, I kept reminding myself that I wasn't *losing* New York. No matter what happens in my life, I have benefited from being there—from the people I met, and the things I learned, and the career advancement that couldn't have happened anywhere else. If and when it is my time to live elsewhere, it'll be an opportunity to add to my life, not subtract from it.

Adaptation: I tried to separate my "what" from my "why." I had done that for my career already; as you might recall, I once felt too attached to my identities as a newspaper reporter or magazine editor, and eventually redefined myself with the sentence, "I tell stories in my own voice." But I hadn't gone through the process *personally*. Who am I, if not the product of the place I live in? I came to a conclusion: "I make the best of any setting."

New Normal: I started to ask: "What is my time in Boulder *for*?" When I look back on it later, what role will it serve my larger life? At first, I thought that Boulder was the place I learned to relax and enjoy the outdoors—and while that's true, it's probably a limited view of things. My time in Boulder, I came to realize, was when I learned that I can go anywhere and thrive. That is a powerfully freeing thing to know.

Wouldn't Go Back: Part of me felt silly returning to Brooklyn—after all, don't I preach the power of *not going back*? But the move back home revealed a nuance to my argument: Change doesn't always have to look like change. Sometimes change is simply permission to do things differently. And that's something I would never want to go back from.

Where I live now, and where I live later, is so much less important than the outcome of this process. Everything, after all, is just the next thing.

You Are Now in the Conscious Cycle

Sometimes, after hearing my perspective on change, someone will ask me whether I believe that all change is good, or whether every new thing is better than the old thing. The answer is no. Logically speaking, that would mean that everything we currently have is crap—because why be happy with anything if a better option is right around the corner? (To see this play out in real life, try being a twenty-something dating in New York. Nobody wants to commit!)

So let me be clear: Not all change is inherently good. Not every new thing is inherently better than the old thing. Opportunities don't just fall into our laps. But while those statements can be true, we must also acknowledge the unstoppable force that is change. It comes whether we want it or not. New things replace old things. They just do. We must accept the inevitability of that—and then move quickly to turn it to our advantage.

Instead of defining ourselves firmly—I am *this*, I do *that*—we must recognize that everything we do, as well as everything we are, is simply the next thing in a long line of next things. *Everything* is the next thing, part of a continuum of successes and failures and doors opening and closing.

You've gone through all this before, of course. Your accomplishments today are due to changes from your past—but you may not have recognized those changes at the time, or you may have been younger and less fearful of them. Cycles of change have come and gone, and because you didn't think of them this way, they did not leave you feeling prepared for the next one.

Here is the opportunity in front of you now: The cycle of change you're currently experiencing can become the Conscious Cycle. This is the cycle in which you're conscious that change is happening, and you're tracking how it shakes and transforms you, and how you can more actively control it as well. This is the cycle where you actively prove to yourself that change can be harnessed to improve your life. It's the cycle you'll remember. And at the end of it, once you reach Wouldn't Go Back, you will have a lesson that guides you forever. You will know that the process works, which means it can work again, which means that, when the cycle starts anew, you can speed past the Panic and move on to the good stuff.

After all, our greatest fortune in life is never to hit pause. It is to have as many tomorrows as possible.

Acknowledgments

"Who truly knew the Figman?"

That was the first sentence of the first book I tried to write, just after college. It was a novel about an outcast named the Figman who started confusing his dreams with his memories, and I wrote it at a time when I thought I'd grow up to be a High-Minded Literary Person. Change taught me otherwise. But look at that—now a very small part of my original effort is appearing in a real book. Just a very different one. So thank you, Figman, for serving the unsung but critical role that something must play in all of our lives: You were the idea that must be explored, before it can be moved on from.

This book, on the other hand, began many years later on a playground in Brooklyn. I was there with my wife and kids, and we got to chatting with Matt Elblonk; our boys had become friendly at school. I told Matt about my podcast, as well as my obsession with how people manage change. He told me this sounds like a book—because, as it turns out, he's a book agent. (This is why I love Brooklyn.) Our families soon became close, and Matt and I talked about this hypothetical book for a few years, and I kept putting it off because frankly the idea of writing it sounded exhausting. Change is hard, I've heard. Then Covid happened, and Matt called me with something halfway between a suggestion and a demand: "Everyone is grappling with change on a massive scale, and now is the time to write that amazing book about change." He was right. I got to work. Thank you, Matt, for being an equally good friend and agent.

I am grateful that this book landed in the capable hands of my editor, Matthew Benjamin, who patiently explained to me how writing a book is not like writing a bunch of magazine articles (which is how my magazine-making instincts drove the earlier drafts). The final result is infinitely better because of him. Thank you also to the Harmony team, Anna Bauer, Luisa Francavilla, Andrea Lau, and Serena Wang. Fact-checking was by Sheri ArbitalJacoby.

Maybe this is the influence of my Jewish mother—who is, of course, always attentive to who must be invited and feel included in every family activity—but my instinct here is to thank literally every friend and colleague who has helped me shape an idea, skill, or experience that helped lead to this book. But that's impractical, and I'll miss too many of you, and it gives me anxiety just thinking about it. So instead, in summary: If you believe I'm talking about you, I am. Thank you.

And now, to narrow in on the making of this book.

Thank you, above all, to everyone who shared their time and their stories with me, and allowed me to then share them in this book. I love entrepreneurs because they see vulnerability as an asset. They're right.

The historical anecdotes in this book often came from research I did for my podcast, which is also called *Build for Tomorrow*. (You should listen!) So many people over the years have contributed their talents to this show: Louis Anslow (aka Pessimists Archive), Alec Balas, Chris Ballew (aka Caspar Babypants), Elisabeth Brier, Chris Kornelis, Britta Lokting, Gia Mora, Mary Pilon, Seth Porges, Jennifer Ridder, Brent

Rose, and James Stewart. Thanks also to Adam Bornstein, Jordan Bornstein, Richelle DeVoe, and Kiki Garthwaite (collectively aka Pen Name) for helping me see the bigger picture. To Marc Andreessen for the early and consequential enthusiasm. And to the team at Stand Together, and Taylor Barkley in particular, for their valuable support.

A lot of the business-focused reporting in this book originated with work I did for *Entrepreneur*. Thanks to the amazing team there, whom I am inspired to work with every day, and with an extra special thanks to Bill Shaw for his steady and encouraging leadership, and the print team who makes miracles happen (past and present: Liz Brody, Jim Clauss, Grant Davis, Frances Dodds, Andre Carter, Tracy Stapp Herold, Monica Im, Jessica Levy Kania, Joe Keohane, Stephanie Makrias, Judith Puckett-Rinella, Paul Scirecalabrisotto, Stephanie Schomer, Eric White).

Thanks to Nicole Lapin, my long-distance work wife and *Hush Money* cohost, whose compliments are gold because she will tell me when something's garbage (but with love). To Jon Bier, for, among his great bounty of advice and generosity, convincing me that I could actually make money speaking onstage. To Adam Soccolich, for figuring out everything I cannot figure out. To Margot Boyer-Dry, for wise and plentiful words. For helping me grow and bring my ideas to life: thanks to Mike Goldberg, Hayden Meyer, and the team at APA; to Charles Yao and the team at The Lavin Agency; to Samantha Bennet and the team at Bulletin; and to Mark Fortier and the team at Fortier PR.

Thanks also to those who have so generously provided time, expertise, insight, friendship, or just plain sanity over the past few years, including Rosie Acosta, James Altucher, George Aye, Christine Bollinger, Sara Cantor, Clint Carter, Mike Darling, Andrew Del-Colle, Cristina Everett, Jeremy Greenberg, Jordan Harbinger, Beth Kaufman, Felicity Kohn, Irina Logra, Tara Mackey, Nick Marino, Terry Rice, Andres Sawicki, Jessica Sawicki, Charna Sherman, Jonathan Smeltser, Lilli Schipper, Tristan Snell, Hala Taha, Kevin Tarasuk, Zander Van Gogh, Jeremy Weintraub, Jay Yow, and more I'm anxious I'm forgetting.

This book was made better by the generous early feedback of Jenny Wood, Taylor Barkley, and Richelle DeVoe. The first draft of this book was written during my family's pandemic displacement in Boulder, Colorado. Thank you to the many great new friends we met there, the coffee shop Dry Storage where I wrote a lot of this book, and to my sister Jodi and her husband, Andy, who made not-home feel like home. And most crucially, thank you to my parents, Barbara and Roy Feifer, who let us occupy their home for eighteen months. But that was no surprise, really: Their support and love has never known bounds, and their excellence in parenting is only surpassed by their ultra-excellence in grandparenting.

Thanks to my sons, Fenn and Collin, who embody the complex grandness of change.

I asked my wife how I should structure these acknowledgments, because she's a book author and has written a few of these before, and she laid out roughly the order of what you just read. "Then you end it with how amazing your wife is," she said, which is good advice, and I am wise to take it, because Jen Miller is indeed amazing, and I am fortunate to share a life with her.

Finally, thank you to *you*—for joining me on whatever part of this journey you have joined. It wouldn't be possible without you.

Index

ABOUT THE AUTHOR

Jason Feifer is the editor in chief of *Entrepreneur* magazine, a keynote speaker, a startup advisor, and a nonstop optimism machine. He is the host of the podcasts *Build for Tomorrow* (yes, same name as this book), which uncovers the surprising solutions to our greatest challenges, and *Problem Solvers*, which helps entrepreneurs overcome any obstacle.

Jason has a unique window into the most innovative minds of today, and he translates those insights into practical lessons for anyone at any stage of their career. He's taught his techniques to executives and employees at companies including Pfizer, Microsoft, Chipotle, DraftKings, and Wix. He has worked as an editor at *Fast Company*, *Men's Health*, and *Boston* magazine, and has written about business and technology for *The Washington Post*, *Slate*, *New York* magazine, and others. Jason is also the coauthor of the novel *Mr. Nice Guy*, a romantic comedy that he wrote with his wife.

To contact Jason, subscribe to his newsletter, and find more resources that can help you build a better future, visit jasonfeifer.com.